Men Love Pies, Girls Like Hummus
by Simon Rimmer

First published in Great Britain in 2013 by Mitchell Beazley,
an imprint of Octopus Publishing Group Limited,
Endeavour House, 189 Shaftesbury Avenue, London WC2H 8JY
www.octopusbooks.co.uk

An Hachette UK Company | www.hachette.co.uk

Copyright © Octopus Publishing Group Limited 2013
Text copyright © Simon Rimmer 2013

ISBN: 978 1 84533 720 9

A CIP catalogue record for this book is
available from the British Library.

Set in Hawksmoor, Minion Pro and Vectora.

Printed and bound in China.

Commissioning Editor Eleanor Maxfield
Deputy Art Director & Designer Yasia Williams-Leedham
Senior Editor Leanne Bryan
Photographer Emma Lee
Illustrator Andrew Berwick
Home Economist Alice Hart
Props Stylist Lesley Dilcock
Copy Editor Jo Richardson
Proofreader Emma Clegg
Indexer Helen Snaith
Production Manager Peter Hunt

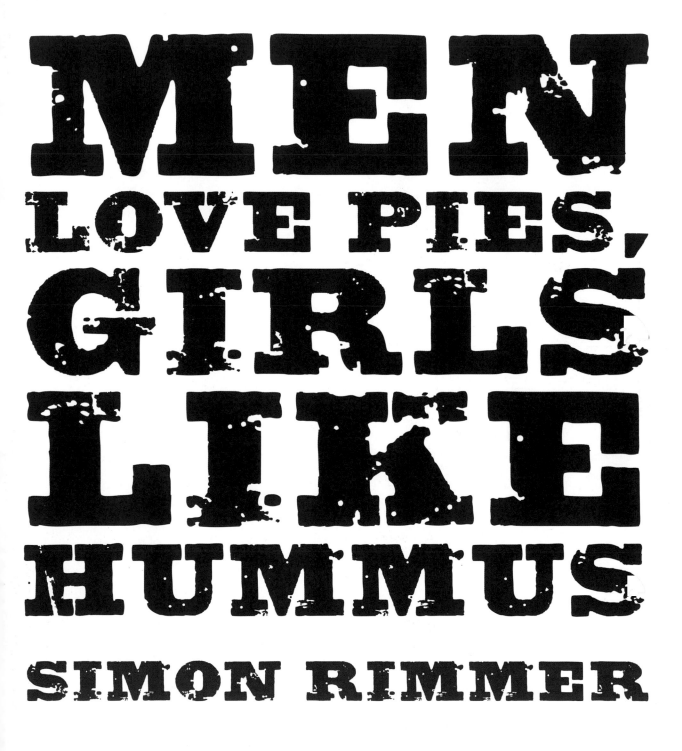

MEN LOVE PIES, GIRLS LIKE HUMMUS

SIMON RIMMER

Mitchell Beazley

CONTENTS

INTRODUCTION

So my little Flo, about three at the time, sits across from me at the Sangam Restaurant in Manchester and asks why is naan bread called naan bread – you know the answer, 'Because nanny loves it'. For years Flo believed that and it still makes me smile. The joy of living a life with food isn't just about the eating; it's the whole nine yards. The people, the facts, the 'not quite' facts, the myths, the legends and the craic.

For example, did you know that vanilla pods come from an orchid? That the word 'avocado' derives from the Aztec word for testicle? That if you put salt on a raw egg it will break down the membrane around the yolk and whisk more evenly? That food looks better in odd numbers? That chocolate was originally a form of currency? That a Danvers Half Long is a type of carrot? That there's an allergy to broad beans called favism, which is prevalent in Sardinia? That my friend put on weight and declared she no longer had a muffin top at the top of her jeans but a full cake stand? That my mate's son thought that the UK Prime Minister was called David Tamarind?

I believe that entire side of life is why I love food so much. When I think back to my childhood, it never stops amazing me just how many memories are related to food. I can't help but smile when I recall the smell of bacon cooked in lard as I'd go into my nan's house, or the delicious creamy taste of the ice cream she used to have. I still wonder what that brand of ice cream was

that came in a big metal tin – feel free to let me know. Not to mention her apple pie with crispy puff pastry, and the crunch of my first Twiglet or the powdery flavour sensation only a Cheese Football can provide.

Then, of course, there are the battles about foods you didn't like as a kid.

Did your mum tell you to eat your crusts so that you'd get lovely curly hair? Mine did… have you seen the photos of me? I'd eat peas with malt vinegar all over 'em and then swallow them whole just so I'd qualify for a slice of my mum's treacle tart. Now my little lad Hamish eats them with Tommy K all over them for the very same reason!

Hamish loves his food. When he was really tiny he'd happily tuck into a spicy curry and get proper curry sweats – I was so proud.

And his love of spice hasn't diminished. His favourite restaurant in London is Bodean's, and a Chilli Dog with extra jalapeños is his idea of heaven. We were in there a while ago and a horrified lady watched this spice-laden 'dog' land in front of my nine year old. She cast a death glare at me, doubtless accusing me of child abuse. I sat back and watched her jaw hit the floor as the wee man scoffed it down with a decent splash of Cholula chilli sauce for good measure.

I've been really lucky over the years that my job has taken me to incredible places and given me the chance to try so many different foods, some good and some

bad. The first time I went to Hong Kong, I was stunned as I turned the corner from my fancy hotel to be in the middle of a small local market. There were cages full of chickens, which were rapidly pulled out and killed for the customer. So many flattened and dried creatures – rabbits, ducks, chickens – and my curiosity forcing me to try chickens' feet (mmmm… chewy, gristly) and a bowl of intestine stew that tasted like having a bad cold! But I loved the fact that my Chinese guide told me that the ethos behind the food was to celebrate difference. We don't have chickens' feet or beaks, so celebrate their difference.

I've eaten most parts of various beasts' bodies – eyes, ears, nose, feet, heart, lung, brain, stomach lining and even testicles. In fact, Sarah Ferguson told me, when I was interviewing her once, that the most unusual thing she's ever had in her mouth was a bull's testicle. Moving on…

In a nutshell, that's the story. This is a book with lots of delicious recipes, obviously, but the chapters are all introduced by stories and anecdotes that have made me smile, laugh and cry over the years. I couldn't have done it without my friends, family and, of course, the random strangers I've eavesdropped on.

Now, before we get into the cooking, I have to point out that the title of the book is NOT meant to cause any arguments between the sexes. It's called *Men Love Pies, Girls Like Hummus* because they are two of the chapters in the book. It doesn't mean…

- If you're female and like pies, you're really a bloke.
- If you're a bloke and like hummus (me), you're really a girl.
- The two chapters can only be read by the appropriate sex.
- If you're a girl and don't like hummus… etc, etc, etc.

One of my mates, after I told him the book title, asked what that made him, as he likes nothing more than a meat and potato pie with a dollop of hummus on top. I know just what that makes you Seb – weird!

There are a good few dishes here that really encourage you to take ownership of the recipe. For instance, if you don't like game very much, then the Game Pie (see page 44) can easily be made with chicken and ham. So please use these very personal recipes as your framework – if you want to add or take away, then do it. Never has a recipe book been so empowering. If you have incredible successes with a new twist, tweet me @simonrim and let me know, then I can steal the idea and use it on a future TV show or in my next book.

I hope you love this book – it's my very best, and I wrote all the words myself in my best handwriting. So, what are you waiting for? Get making pies, eating hummus... and the pastries are definitely assumed.

Simon Rimmer

When I was 16 (frighteningly over 30 years ago), I was fed up at school and didn't really want to stay on and do A levels. At the same time my dad was made redundant and fancied working for himself. So I found a little shop in the middle of Chester and suggested to my dad that we set up a sandwich shop doing handmade butties, which you could sit in and eat or take away. I also said we could make great coffee like we'd had in Italy. I got all fired up about this until my dad uttered the now classic quote, **'You'll never make money out of sandwiches'**, as I'm sure Marks and Spencer, Pret A Manger and the like would agree… NOT! Love you Dad. So here's some great butties that Rimmer and Son would have produced.

RARE BEEF WITH RED ONION & CHILLI JAM ON CHARRED OLIVE BREAD

Feeds 4–6

450g (1lb) piece of beef fillet
vegetable oil, for rubbing
salt and black pepper
1 loaf of olive bread
olive oil, for brushing

Red onion and chilli jam

olive oil, for frying
4 red onions, finely sliced
1 garlic clove, sliced
1 (or 2 if you're really brave) red bird's
  eye chillies
100ml (3½fl oz) red wine vinegar
125g (4½oz) demerara sugar
salt and black pepper

To serve

about 4 tbsp good-quality mayonnaise
handful of rocket or watercress

The mere mention of rare beef and chilli makes me salivate – it's my Pavlov's dog reaction, and I can feel myself growling and baring my teeth as I type, longing for the succulent, chewy meat to be torn apart by my canine teeth and then yelp as the fiery jam hits me… grrrrrrrrrrrr.

1 Preheat the oven to 220°C/fan 200°C/gas mark 7.

2 Let the beef come up to room temperature, then rub with vegetable oil, season well and cook in a very hot frying pan until browned and sealed on all sides and both ends.

3 Transfer the beef to a roasting tray and pop into the oven for 12–15 minutes to finish cooking, then remove from the oven and rest for at least 8 minutes (it's also delicious if left until completely cold).

4 Meanwhile, for the jam, heat a little olive oil in a saucepan and gently fry the onion, garlic and chilli for at least 10 minutes until soft and sweet. Add the vinegar and sugar, crank up the heat and boil for about 5–6 minutes to thicken to a jam, then simmer for 10 minutes more. Season well, then leave to cool.

5 Cut thick doorstops of the olive bread and brush with olive oil on both sides. Place on a hot griddle pan and cook for about 2 minutes on each side to char.

6 To serve, spread a little mayo on each piece of bread, then add some rocket or watercress. Slice the delicious beef and sit that on top, add a spoonful of the fiery jam, then pop the other piece of bread on top and eat like a rabid dog.

PORK MEATBALL SUB WITH RAW TOMATO SAUCE

There's something really wrong about hot meatballs in a sandwich… but wrong in a good way! It's impossible to eat them without wearing them, it's impossible to eat them without looking and sounding like a 6-year-old kid and it's impossible to stop eating them and wanting them.

1 To make the meatballs, beat the eggs and milk together in a bowl, then add everything else (except the oil) including seasoning. Mix well with your hands and mould into balls about 2.5–3cm (2–1¼in) in diameter. Chill for 20 minutes.

2 Fry the balls in a little vegetable oil in a frying pan over a medium heat for about 8 minutes until cooked through, turning to brown and cook evenly.

3 Meanwhile, for the sauce, heat a little olive oil in a saucepan and fry the onion, celery and garlic for about 5 minutes until soft. Add the stock and boil to reduce by two-thirds. Take off the heat, add the tomatoes and stir well, then season well.

4 To serve, slice the subs lengthways in half. Sit a few meatballs along the length of each bottom half, spoon over the sauce and top with Parmesan shavings, then add the top half of each sub and devour.

Makes 8 subs

Pork meatballs

2 large eggs
125ml (4fl oz) milk
450g (1lb) minced pork
200g (7oz) breadcrumbs (any sort)
75g (2¾oz) Parmesan cheese, grated
1 garlic clove, crushed
salt and black pepper
vegetable oil, for frying

Raw tomato sauce

olive oil, for frying
1 onion, finely diced
2 celery sticks, finely chopped
1 garlic clove, finely chopped
150ml (¼ pint) chicken stock
about 12 plum tomatoes, finely chopped
salt and black pepper

To serve

8 soft white sub rolls
Parmesan cheese shavings

DUCK À L'ORANGE ON TOAST

Feeds 4

2 duck breasts, about 200g (7oz) each
salt and black pepper
4 slices of brioche
3 figs, cut into rounds
75g (2¾oz) butter
1 tbsp demerara sugar
watercress, to garnish

Orange sauce

75g (2¾oz) caster sugar
50ml (2fl oz) white wine vinegar
2 oranges, rind finely grated, then
flesh peeled and cut into rounds
125ml (4fl oz) orange liqueur

I'm conscious that an awful lot of the recipes in this book seem to be looking back at things I loved as a kid. Duck à l'Orange is a real *Abigails's Party* kind of a dish – slightly naff, aspiring to be something it isn't and with the potential to be awful! This lovely 'sandwich', however, is a stormer. The sweetness of the sauce, the sugar on the bread and then a kick of vinegar, the lovely fatty duck and suddenly you're at a cool party where everyone's listening to '70s tunes in an ironic way wearing equally ironic cheesecloth shirts and flares… yeah, groovy!

1 Preheat the oven to 200°C/fan 180°C/gas mark 6.

2 Season the duck, then place skin-side down in a cold pan. Turn on the heat to medium-high and cook for 8 minutes, tipping away but reserving the fat. Flip over and cook on the other side for 2 minutes to seal.

3 Transfer the duck to a roasting tray, skin-side up, and roast for 6 minutes if you like it pink; a few minutes longer if you prefer it more well done. Remove from the oven and rest for a few minutes.

4 Meanwhile, toast the brioche under a hot grill. Lay the fig rounds on top, dot with the butter and sprinkle with the demerara sugar, then grill until caramelized.

5 For the sauce, put the caster sugar and vinegar in a saucepan and boil for 3–4 minutes until sticky, then stir in the orange rind. Add the orange rounds and the booze and cook for 5 minutes, then stir in a little of the skimmed reserved duck fat.

6 Carve the duck and divide between the toast. Spoon over the sauce, then garnish with a little watercress. Et voilà!

DUCK BURGER

I suppose the ultimate 'sandwich' these days has to be the burger. Wherever you go you'll find burgers on menus, whether it's a fast food joint, a pub or even a fancy restaurant. We sell loads of burgers at EARLE and as a result we like to play around with variations on the theme. This fella has proved to be a very popular addition to our portfolio, and is really nice served with Thai-style prawn crackers on the side.

1 Preheat the oven to 200°C/fan 180°C/gas mark 6.

2 Pulse the confit duck leg meat in a food processor until smoothish, then pop into a bowl. Do the same with the breasts, but chop them first.

3 Add the breadcrumbs, spring onions, parsley, garlic, egg and seasoning and mix well with your hands, then mould into 4 burgers.

4 Brush the burgers on both sides with oil and cook in a hot frying or griddle pan, or under a hot grill, turning halfway through, for 6–8 minutes until sealed all over. Transfer to a baking tray and cook in the oven for 4–6 minutes until cooked through.

5 To serve, sit the burgers in the toasted buns, sprinkle over the cucumber, coriander and plum sauce and eat.

Makes 4 burgers

meat from 2 confit duck legs (see page 37)
2 duck breasts, about 200g (7oz) each, skinned
125g (4½oz) breadcrumbs (any sort)
50g (¾oz) spring onions, finely chopped
1 tbsp chopped parsley
1 garlic clove, crushed
1 large egg, beaten
salt and black pepper
vegetable oil, for brushing

To serve
4 sesame-seed burger buns, toasted and split in half
½ cucumber, finely diced
handful of coriander leaves
few tbsp Chinese plum sauce

17

SANTA FE CHICKEN CAESAR WRAP WITH HOT SAUCE

Makes 8 wraps

4 skinless chicken breasts, about 200g (7oz) each

vegetable oil, for brushing

salt and black pepper

1 head of Cos lettuce, shredded

1 red onion, finely sliced

100g (3½oz) drained canned red kidney beans, rinsed

1 tbsp chopped coriander leaves

8 soft corn tortillas

your favourite hot sauce (mine is Cholula), to serve

Caesar dressing

100g (3½oz) Parmesan cheese, grated

1 tsp capers

3 salted anchovy fillets

2 tbsp white wine vinegar

1 garlic clove, crushed

250g (9oz) mayonnaise

30g (1oz) Dijon mustard

salt and black pepper

I filmed in Mexico a few years back and fell in love with the soft corn tortillas over there, which are so much yummier than the wheat ones we normally buy over here. However, those work just dandy in this recipe. The key to 'wrapping' is to avoid the big fat lump of dough at the bottom, so don't be afraid to trim your wraps to create foodie dovetails and make the end result a work of craftsmanship.

1 Preheat the oven to 200°C/fan 180°C/gas mark 6.

2 Brush the chicken breasts with oil and season well, then cook in a hot griddle pan for 3 minutes on each side to char. Transfer to a baking tray and bake in the oven for about 20 minutes until cooked through. Remove from the oven and leave to cool.

3 Now for the dressing – the ingredients make much more than you'll need, but it's so delicious that you'll be spreading the rest on your toast in the morning. In a food processor, blend the Parmesan, capers, anchovies, vinegar and garlic together until smooth. Now mix in the mayo, mustard and seasoning (if the dressing seems a bit thick, then add a little water, as you want a thick, creamy consistency). Keep cool.

4 Put the lettuce, onion, beans and coriander in a bowl, then add the dressing a spoonful at a time and shake the bowl to dress. When you have added enough dressing to coat the ingredients well, just quickly toss it with your hands.

5 Put a generous line of salady stuff down the middle of each tortilla (feel free to warm them first), then slice the chicken and divide it between the wraps. Splash on the hot sauce, wrap up, trim and dovetail, then eat before a well-deserved siesta.

ROASTED PORTOBELLO MUSHROOMS WITH SPINACH, NUTMEG & FETA ON SOURDOUGH

Feeds 4

4 large or 8 medium Portobello
  mushrooms

salt and black pepper

1 tbsp olive oil, plus extra for drizzling

2 garlic cloves, finely sliced

few sprigs of thyme

15g (½oz) butter

1 onion, finely diced

250g (9oz) bag baby spinach

1 tsp freshly grated nutmeg

175g (6oz) Greek feta cheese,
  finely cubed or crumbled

1 large egg, beaten

100g (3½oz) mayonnaise

1 tbsp Dijon mustard

1 sourdough loaf, cut into 1cm
  (½in) thick slices – a bit bigger
  than the mushrooms

sliced tomato or gherkin
  (optional)

fresh tomato salad or chips,
  to serve

In all my time of owning Greens, I've tried to perfect the ultimate veggie burger. I want to create something with texture, chewiness and flavour to match, but to this day I've not managed it. The closest thing I've come up with for taste is to use Portobello mushrooms. Some places would call this a 'burger' – it's not, but it is bloody tasty.

1 Preheat the oven to 200°C/fan 180°C/gas mark 6.

2 Take the stems off the mushrooms, then sit them on a baking tray, gill-side up. Season, drizzle with olive oil and lay a slice of garlic on each one, then some thyme. Roast for about 12 minutes until tender.

3 Meanwhile, melt the butter with the oil in a frying or sauté pan and fry the onion gently for about 5 minutes until soft. Add the spinach and cook for 3–4 minutes to wilt it. Now add the nutmeg. Remove from the heat and drain off any excess liquid.

4 Put into a bowl with the feta and mix well, then add the egg and mix again.

5 Divide the mixture between the mushrooms and return to the oven for 5 minutes more to set.

6 Beat the mayo and mustard together. Toast, griddle or just cut the bread. Spread the mayo mixture on to half the bread slices (at this point feel free to add sliced tomato or gherkin), sit the mushrooms on top, then top with the remaining pieces of bread. This is particularly nice with a fresh tomato salad if you feel righteous, or with loads of chips if you don't.

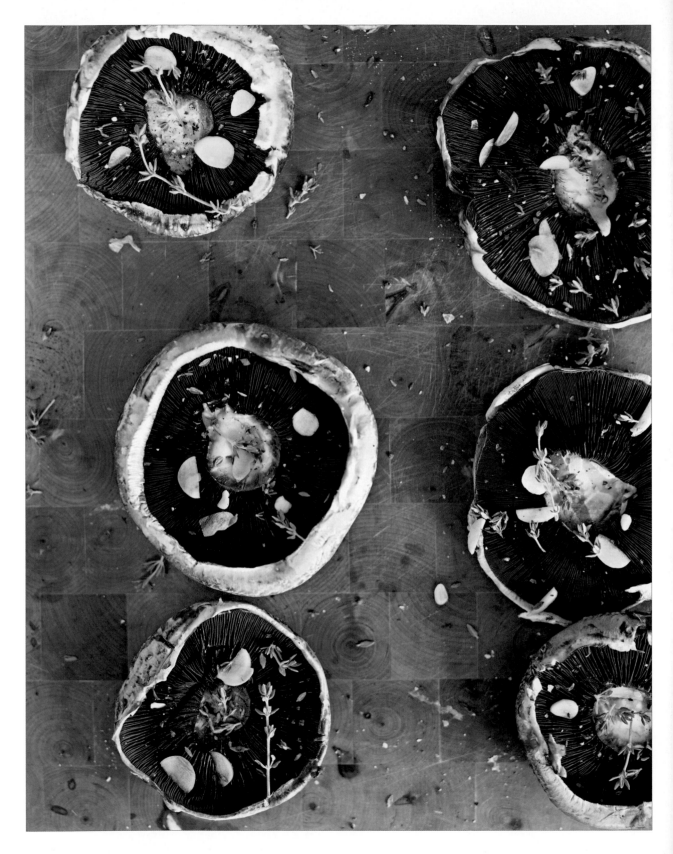

My mate Martin Holland and I were out having a few bevvies one night and, as ever, the talk turned to food. Martin was asking me what kind of things I cooked for my wife Ali, and also what kind of things I'd cook to impress a girl, if I was single that is. I started listing a few dishes and then Martin pipes up, **'Of course, girls like hummus'**. It made me laugh out loud, so this chapter is full of recipes to cook for the ladies in your life, even if that's your mum and your sister or if you're a girl too. All of them have been tested in my restaurants and at home, and are basically dishes that have sold well and been described as favourites by female customers, friends and family.

MINT & PINE NUT HUMMUS

Have you noticed how hummus has become a bit of a hybrid these days? Go into any supermarket and you'll find every kind of hummus, from peri-peri through Moroccan spiced to caramelized onion, and I love 'em all. Obviously, with the title of this book, I think I'm likely to be named as the Hummus Tsar at the next government reshuffle. In the meantime, this is a lovely one, fresh and zesty with a simple flatbread to go with it – if you can, eat the bread when it's warm.

Feeds 6

400g can chickpeas, drained and rinsed
1 garlic clove, crushed
1 bunch of mint, chopped
100ml (3½fl oz) extra virgin olive oil
finely grated rind and juice of 2 lemons
1 tbsp tahini
1 tbsp toasted pine nuts

Flatbread

150ml (¼ pint) water
10g (¼oz) dried yeast
250g (9oz) natural yogurt
550g (1lb 4oz) strong white flour, plus extra for dusting
pinch of salt
1 green chilli, finely chopped
40ml (1½fl oz) olive oil, plus extra for brushing

1 In a food processor, blend the chickpeas, garlic and mint until smooth (if you want to be fancy, put a quarter of the chickpeas aside, then fold in whole for a cosmopolitan hummus), then add everything else for the hummus and pulse together.

2 For the flatbread, bring the water to the boil. Meanwhile, combine the yeast with the yogurt in a bowl. Pour over the boiling water and stir it well.

3 Add 250g (9oz) of the flour and combine well with your hands. Cover and leave to prove for 25 minutes.

4 Add the salt, chilli, oil and the rest of the flour and give this a really good mix, then cover and leave to prove again for an hour – it should just about double in size.

5 Knock the dough back by bashing it on your work surface, then divide it into 6 and roll into balls. Roll out each ball on a lightly floured surface to about 3mm (⅛in) thick.

6 Brush the bread on both sides with a little oil and cook in a hot frying pan or griddle pan for about 30 seconds on each side. Serve the flatbread warm with the hummus.

ARTICHOKE, PEA & BUTTERNUT SQUASH SALAD

Feeds 4–6

2 butternut squash
vegetable oil, for roasting
3 garlic cloves, peeled
salt and black pepper
olive oil, for frying
1 onion, sliced
150g (5½oz) cooked fresh or frozen peas
280g jar chargrilled artichokes in olive oil, drained
handful of watercress
1 tbsp capers
flatbread, grilled or griddled until crispy, to serve

Harissa dressing

2 tbsp harissa paste
handful of mint
handful of parsley
100ml (3½fl oz) sherry vinegar
250ml (9fl oz) extra virgin olive oil
salt and black pepper
pinch of caster sugar (optional)

If you've ever tried to prep an artichoke, you'll know it's a right pain, pulling off leaves, trimming, sitting in acidulated water etc, etc. Don't get me wrong, they're delicious, but you've gotta lot of time to commit to. So this lovely salad uses the griddled fellas out of a jar and all the hard work is done for you, which means you can prepare the rest of the dish to perfection.

1 Preheat the oven to 200°C/fan 180°C/gas mark 6.

2 Peel the squash and scoop out the seeds, then cut into 3cm (1¼in) cubes, trimming away all the irregular bits so that you have pretty cubes.

3 Heat a good glug of vegetable oil in a roasting tray in the oven, then add the squash and garlic, season and toss in the oil. Roast for about 30 minutes until soft. Leave to cool a bit.

4 Meanwhile, heat a splash of olive oil in a frying or sauté pan and slowly fry the onion over a low heat for about 30 minutes until caramelized. Leave to cool while you make the dressing.

5 In a food processor, blend the harissa, mint, parsley, vinegar and (once roasted) the garlic together. With the motor running, add the extra virgin olive oil in a steady stream. Taste, season and add the sugar if the dressing is too sharp.

6 To serve, gently toss the squash, onion, peas, artichokes, watercress and capers together, then toss with some of the dressing (you'll have lots of it, so add as much or as little as you want). Serve with crispy flatbread.

CRISPY OYSTER MUSHROOM SALAD

I've always liked the warm ingredients in a salad thing. This works brilliantly well, the warm, crispy mushrooms bringing the plum dressing to life (you can use plum sauce for the base of the dressing if you can't get any decent plums). If you can't imagine the flavours, think of a crispy duck texture and taste with all the other goodies.

Feeds 4

150g (5½oz) Chinese five-spice powder
100g (3½oz) plain flour
pinch of salt
400g (14oz) oyster mushrooms
vegetable oil, for deep-frying
sea salt, for sprinkling
about 250g (9oz) watercress
1 cucumber, deseeded, cut into batons
1 tbsp pickled ginger
12 spring onions, shredded
handful of coriander leaves

Plum dressing

1 red chilli, finely chopped
1 star anise
100ml (3½fl oz) rice vinegar
juice of 1 lime
100g (3½oz) caster sugar
200g (7oz) plums, finely chopped
75ml (2½fl oz) olive oil

1 For the plum dressing, put the chilli, star anise, vinegar, lime juice and sugar in a saucepan. Bring to the boil and cook for about 3–4 minutes until syrupy.

2 Take the pan off the heat, add the plums and stir well, then whisk in the olive oil. You can pass the dressing through a sieve, but I like it chunky.

3 Combine the five-spice, flour and salt in a dish. Tear the mushrooms into strips and coat well in the spice mixture, then shake off the excess.

4 Half-fill a deep-fat fryer or deep, heavy-based saucepan with vegetable oil and heat to 180°C, or until a small cube of bread tossed into the oil turns golden in about 30 seconds. Deep-fry the mushies, in batches, for about 5 minutes until crisp. Remove with a slotted spoon and drain on kitchen paper, then sprinkle on a little sea salt.

5 Assemble the salad by tossing the watercress and cucumber in a little of the dressing, then add the ginger and spring onions. Top with the mushies and more dressing, then the coriander leaves.

SOLE FILLETS WRAPPED AROUND BABY VEG WITH LEMON MUSTARD SAUCE

This is a dish to impress – it looks like you've been working your butt off all day, when in reality it's a quick job. If you can't get baby veg, then just finely slice the grown-up size. I don't think this needs anything with it, but feel free to prove me wrong… again!

1 Lay the sole fillets on a board and season well.

2 Put the carrots and asparagus in a saucepan of boiling water and blanch for 1–2 minutes. Drain well.

3 Arrange a mixture of the blanched veg on one end of each fillet, roll up and secure with a cocktail stick. Sit on an oiled saucer inside a steamer. Squeeze over the lemon juice and steam for 4 minutes until the sole is just cooked.

4 Meanwhile, for the sauce, put the wine in a saucepan and simmer until reduced by half. Add the cream and cook for 3–4 minutes to thicken slightly. Add the butter, mustard and lemon juice and whisk to combine (be careful not to overheat). Season and add the parsley.

5 Serve the sole fillets with the sauce poured over.

Feeds 4

4 sole fillets, cut in half
salt and black pepper
2–3 baby carrots, finely sliced
8 mini asparagus spears, finely sliced
vegetable oil, for oiling
juice of ½ lemon

Lemon mustard sauce
90ml (3fl oz) white wine
125ml (4fl oz) double cream
20g (¾oz) butter
1 tbsp Dijon mustard
juice of 1 lemon
salt and black pepper
1 tbsp chopped parsley

BABY SQUID & POTATO SALAD

Feeds 4

400g (14oz) cleaned baby squid tubes
150ml (¼ pint) milk
200g (7oz) panko breadcrumbs
1 tsp dried chilli flakes
vegetable oil, for deep-frying

Potato salad

250g (9oz) cooked fine egg noodles
250g (9oz) cubed golden sweet potato, boiled until tender and drained
about 12 SunBlush tomatoes
4 spring onions, finely chopped
1 tbsp pumpkin seeds
1 tsp black onion seeds
1 tbsp chopped mint

Ginger and lime dressing

150ml (¼pint) olive oil
juice of 2 limes
2 tbsp sherry vinegar
1 tbsp plus 2 tsp fresh ginger juice
1 tbsp sesame oil
1 red chilli, finely chopped
salt and black pepper

Squid is an acquired taste, and it's tricky to get it right: cook it too slowly and it turns to rubber; cook it too fast and the same thing happens. But, when it's right – well, it's pretty darn good. This is a dish that I reckon has about a 75 per cent female fan base in EARLE. It's not too heavy yet it packs a decent punch and, so I'm told, it's perfect with pink Champagne and ice-cold Sauvignon Blanc… and nice shoes.

1 Cut the squid tubes down one side, then score the inside with a knife in a crisscross pattern. Cut into strips about 5mm (¼in) wide.

2 Put the milk in a dish and the combine the crumbs and chilli flakes in a separate dish. Dip the squid strips in the milk, then in the crumb mix to coat.

3 Half-fill a deep-fat fryer or deep, heavy-based saucepan with vegetable oil and heat to 160°C, or until a small cube of bread tossed into the oil turns golden in about 45 seconds. Deep-fry the squid, in batches, for about 3 minutes until crisp and golden. Remove with a slotted spoon and drain on kitchen paper.

4 For the salad, cut the cooked noodles into 5–7.5cm (2–3in) pieces, then put in a bowl with all the other salad ingredients except the mint.

5 Put all the dressing ingredients in a bottle and shake well, then season.

6 Dress the salad, then add the mint. Serve with the crispy squid on top.

CORONATION PRAWN VOL-AU-VENTS

Makes 6 vol-au-vents

350g (12oz) ready-made puff pastry

beaten egg, to glaze

15g (½oz) butter

50g (1¾oz) plain flour, plus extra
  for dusting

200ml (7fl oz) warm fish stock

1 tbsp curry paste, thinned with a little
  hot water

salt and black pepper

1 large egg yolk

75ml (2½fl oz) double cream

18 cooked peeled king prawns

1 tbsp flaked almonds

3 spring onions, chopped

I remember going to a party at my grandparents' house when I was little. The food still has an effect on me now. I recall seeing whole dressed salmon, caviar, slices of meat the likes of which I'd never seen before – a whole table full of stuff that I didn't recognise. But the very best thing in the whole world on that night of discovery was the VOL-AU-VENT! From the first taste of the warm, crisp pastry, giving way to a creamy filling… it was like a pasty that had been inhabited by an angel. In recent times, the old VAV has been very popular at EARLE parties, and at a particular birthday bash for a lovely group of girls the vol-au-vents were devoured in minutes, so we made 'em some more… gentlemen us!

1 Preheat the oven to 200°C/fan 180°C/gas mark 6.

2 Roll out the puff pastry on a lightly floured work surface to about 3mm (⅛in) thick, then cut out 12 circles about 10cm (4in) in diameter. Cut a smaller circle out of the centre of 6 of them and discard.

3 Lay the 6 complete circles on a floured baking tray, brush with beaten egg, then sit a circle with a hole in on top of each. Bake for about 15 minutes until crisp, golden and dry, then remove from the oven and turn the oven down to 180°C/fan 160°C/gas mark 4.

4 Meanwhile, melt the butter in a saucepan, add the flour and stir until a roux (smooth paste) forms. Remove from heat and beat in the warm fish stock and curry paste a little at a time. Return to the heat, season and bring to the boil, then simmer for 10 minutes, stirring all the time.

5 Beat the egg yolk and cream together, then beat this mixture into the sauce. Stir in the prawns, almonds and spring onions.

6 Spoon the prawn mixture into the cooked pastry cases and bake for another 10 minutes. Serve with ironic retro smiles.

CRAB TART WITH FRESH MOOLI SALAD

Just to show that all pies/pastry dishes don't have to be heavy and stodgy, this is a delicate little beauty. A light, crunchy pastry case filled with a spicy, lemony crab filling and served with a fresh mooli salad. You can serve this cold, though lovely and warm is the best way, if I'm honest. It also works as six individual tarts, but I prefer one big one, and would eat it all on my own given the chance.

Feeds 6

225g (8oz) plain flour, plus extra for dusting
75g (2¾oz) butter, chilled and cubed
pinch of salt
50ml (2fl oz) milk
1 large egg yolk

Crab filling

2 large eggs
2 large egg yolks
400ml (14fl oz) double cream
salt and black pepper
450g (1lb) cooked white crabmeat
6 spring onions, finely chopped
1 tbsp drained canned sweetcorn kernels
1 tsp dried chilli flakes
finely grated rind and juice of 1 lemon

Mooli salad

5cm (2in) piece of fresh root ginger
100ml (3½fl oz) groundnut or walnut oil
50ml (2fl oz) rice vinegar
juice of 2 limes
1 tbsp light soy sauce
1 large mooli, peeled and finely grated

1 For the pastry, pulse the flour, butter and salt in a food processor until 'crumby'. Add the milk and egg yolk and pulse until a dough forms.

2 Knead the dough on a lightly floured surface for a few minutes, then cover and chill for at least an hour.

3 When you're ready to use the dough, preheat the oven to 180°C/fan 160°C/gas mark 4.

4 Roll out the dough on a lightly floured surface – you'll get a piece big enough to line one 22.5cm (9in) tart tin or 6 little ones. Trim the edges and prick the base/s all over with a fork. Line the pastry case/s with greaseproof paper, fill with dried beans or rice and 'blind bake' the large one for 20–25 minutes or the small ones for about 15 minutes until just cooked and dry but still pale.

5 Meanwhile, for the filling, beat the whole eggs, yolks and cream together in a bowl and season well. Fold in the crab, spring onions, sweetcorn, chilli flakes and lemon rind and juice, then mix together well.

6 Remove the paper and beans or rice from the tart case/s, then fill the large tart case with the crab mixture or divide it between the 6 small tart cases. Bake the large case for about 20 minutes or the small ones for about 15 minutes until set and golden brown.

7 For the salad, peel and finely grate the ginger, then whisk with the oil, vinegar, lime juice and soy. Toss the grated mooli in the dressing. Serve alongside the warm tarts.

Feeds 4

4 skinless chicken breasts, about 200g (7oz) each, a few slashes cut into the surface

Lime marinade

finely grated rind and juice of 6 limes

stems from 1 bunch of coriander, chopped

1 garlic clove, sliced

50ml (2fl oz) olive oil

1 tbsp clear honey

salt and pepper

Radish and pickled ginger salad

90ml (3fl oz) vegetable oil

1 tbsp sesame oil

1 tbsp rice vinegar

salt and black pepper

about 200g (7oz) radishes, trimmed and sliced

100g (3½oz) pickled ginger

1 tbsp sesame seeds

a few baby salad leaves, such as chard and rocket

LIME-MARINATED CHICKEN

I crave this dish when I want to eat healthily… well, I WANT to do that all the time, but there are too many temptations in my life to indulge in! It's a very simple dish that I'll either have with nothing added, if I'm dropping carbs, or with a big plate of sticky rice if I'm not.

1 Mix all the marinade ingredients together. Put in a sealable plastic food bag, add the chicken and seal, then massage the marinade into the meat. Put the bag in the fridge overnight and forget about it.

2 When you're ready to cook the chicken, preheat the oven to 200°C/fan 180°C/gas mark 6.

3 Transfer all the bag's contents to an ovenproof dish, cover with foil and roast for about 25 minutes, or until the chicken is cooked through.

4 Meanwhile, for the salad, make the dressing by whisking the oils and vinegar together in a bowl, then season. Toss in all the other ingredients except the leaves.

5 To serve, I like to slice the chicken, then assemble the salad in a pile, dipping the tender leaves in the dressing as I go.

CONFIT DUCK WITH BEAN GRATIN

Feeds 4

2 tbsp olive oil

2 shallots, finely chopped

2 celery sticks, finely diced

1 red pepper, cored, deseeded and diced

2 x 400g cans mixed beans, drained and rinsed

50g (1¾oz) crème fraîche

1 tbsp grain mustard

Confit duck

150g (5½oz) coarse sea salt

4 duck legs

50ml (2fl oz) Calvados

12 garlic cloves, peeled

few sprigs of thyme and rosemary

about 800g (1lb 12oz) goose fat

2 bay leaves

few twists of black pepper

Parmesan crust

100g (3½oz) fresh breadcrumbs

100g (3½oz) Parmesan cheese, finely grated

75g (2¾oz) butter, melted

salt and black pepper

I'm going to show you how to make a simple confit for the duck, but if you want to save time, this will work with canned duck confit – if you ever go to France, it's one of the best things to buy in volume in supermarkets.

1 To make the confit duck, rub the sea salt all over the duck legs, then put them into an ovenproof dish with a lid (not too big – the legs should be a tightish fit). Pour over the Calvados, then chop up one of the garlic cloves and sprinkle that and half the thyme and rosemary sprigs over the top. Cover and marinate in the fridge for 4 hours, or overnight if possible.

2 Remove the duck from the fridge and brush off as much of the salty marinade as possible. Wipe out the dish with kitchen paper, then return the duck to the dish. Preheat the oven to 150°C/fan 130°C/gas mark 2.

3 Melt the goose fat in a saucepan and add the remaining thyme and rosemary sprigs, garlic and the bay. Pour the fat and herbs over the duck and season with black pepper. Cover the dish and bake for 3–4 hours, then remove from the oven and set aside to cool.

4 When you're ready to prepare the gratin, preheat the oven to 200°C/fan 180°C/gas mark 6. Scrape most of the set fat off the duck legs, then roast them in an ovenproof dish for about 30 minutes until crisp.

5 Meanwhile, combine all the crust ingredients in a bowl.

6 Heat the oil in a saucepan and gently fry the shallots, celery and red pepper for about 5 minutes until soft. Add the beans, crème fraîche and mustard, then simmer for a further 5 minutes.

7 Divide the bean mixture between 4 flameproof bowls, top with the crust and cook under a hot grill for 3–4 minutes until crisp and golden. Serve with a duck leg on top of each bowl.

MEN
LOVE
PIES

The ravages of time do nothing for our faces and bodies – the older we get, the more careful we have to be about what we eat. The days of wolfing down a kebab and chips after eight pints and not putting an ounce of weight on are long gone for me. One day I was on a train going to London listening to two older ladies talking about weight problems. They chatted on and one of them revealed that her husband was carrying a few extra pounds, not for any reason other than the fact that 'men love pies' – me too! This will be the most used chapter in the book.

BEEF & ONION PIE WITH CREAM CHEESE PASTRY

Feeds 4–6

225g (8oz) butter, chilled and cubed
100g (3½oz) cream cheese
4 tbsp double cream
300g (10½oz) plain flour, plus extra
  for dusting
pinch of salt
beaten egg, to glaze

Beef filling

vegetable oil, for frying
450g (1lb) good-quality minced
  beef steak
1 onion, finely diced
1 carrot, finely diced
1 garlic clove, crushed
1 tbsp tomato purée
few sprigs of thyme
200ml (7fl oz) Madeira
200ml (7fl oz) strong beef or
  game stock
salt and black pepper
vegetables of your choice and brown
  sauce, to serve

I was having lunch with my agent, Anne, at Dean Street Townhouse in Soho a while ago. We'd had a full-on morning of meetings and discussions about various projects, laughing, arguing and chatting with each other and other people, and we decided it was food time. When the menu came I was overjoyed at the appearance of mince and potatoes on it. It was bloody delicious – rich, warming and comforting – and I didn't speak for the whole period I was eating... so Anne now thinks I should eat it all the time! With that as my inspiration, I'm going to top it with a delicious cream cheese pastry that's easy to make and is very forgiving for the inexperienced cook.

1 Pulse the butter, cream cheese and cream together in a food processor until combined – don't over-do it. Add the flour and salt and pulse to just combine. Cover and chill in the fridge for at least 30 minutes.

2 For the filling, heat a little oil in a sauté pan or saucepan and fry the mince, stirring it and breaking it up, until browned. Remove from the pan.

3 Add bit more oil to the pan and gently fry the onion, carrot and garlic until softened but not coloured. Return the mince to the pan, add the tomato purée and cook for 4–5 minutes to remove the bitterness.

4 Add the thyme, Madeira, stock and seasoning and bring to the boil, then simmer for at least 30 minutes. Spoon the filling into a 20cm (8in) round, deep pie dish and leave to cool.

5 Preheat the oven to 200°C/fan 180°C/gas mark 6.

6 Cut the pastry into a third and two-thirds. Roll out the larger piece on a floured surface to a round just bigger than your pie dish. From the other piece of pastry, roll a strip long enough to go around the rim of the pie dish.

7 Brush the rim of the dish with beaten egg and press the long strip of dough around the rim. Brush the dough with beaten egg and lay the round piece of pastry on top of this, pressing around the edge to seal. Trim any extra pastry from the edge, then brush the top with beaten egg and cut a couple of slits in the pastry so that the steam can escape.

8 Bake for about 25 minutes until crisp and golden, then serve with your fave veggies and brown sauce.

SHEPHERD'S PIE WITH CAULIFLOWER CHEESE TOP

This recipe, like many others, really came about by accident. It's another 'staff meal' success. Make a shepherd's pie… tick; have some veg with it… tick; save on washing up and oven space by combining the two… big fat tick. Tasty… beyond tasty!

1 Heat a little oil in a frying or sauté pan and fry the minced lamb, stirring and breaking it up, until browned. Remove from the pan.

2 Add a bit more oil to the pan and gently fry the onion, carrot and garlic for 8 minutes until soft. Return the minced lamb to the pan, add the tomato purée and cook for 6 minutes to remove the bitterness.

3 Stir in the stock and bring the mixture to boil, then turn the heat down and simmer for 40 minutes.

4 Meanwhile, cook the potato in a saucepan of salted boiling water until tender, then drain well, return to the pan and mash with the butter.

5 Blanch the cauliflower florets in a saucepan of salted boiling water for 2 minutes, then drain.

6 Preheat the oven to 200°C/fan 180°C/gas mark 6.

7 Beat the crème fraîche, mustard, egg and Cheddar together in a bowl, then fold in the cauliflower florets.

8 Put the lamb mixture into a 20cm (8in) square baking dish, top with the mash and then spoon over the cauliflower mixture.

9 Bake for 20 minutes, then finish it off under a hot grill to bubble the cheese. Serve with green veggies.

Feeds 4 ordinary humans or 2 greedy chefs

vegetable oil, for frying
450g (1lb) minced lamb
1 onion, finely diced
1 carrot, finely diced
1 garlic clove, crushed
2 tbsp tomato purée
200ml (7fl oz) strong lamb stock
1 tbsp chopped parsley
green vegetables, to serve

Cauliflower cheese topping
150g (5½oz) potato, peeled and cut into even-sized pieces
75g (2¾oz) butter
250g (9oz) cauliflower florets
150g (5½oz) crème fraîche
1 tbsp Dijon mustard
1 large egg
150g (5½oz) strong mature Cheddar cheese
salt

GAME PIE

Feeds 4

450g (1lb) plain flour, plus extra
 for dusting
salt and black pepper
50ml (2fl oz) milk
50ml (2fl oz) water
150g (5½oz) lard, chopped
beaten egg yolk, to glaze

Game filling

450g (1lb) pork sausagemeat
2 guinea fowl breasts, skinned and
 cut into large chunks
225g (8oz) boneless, skinless
 duck, cut into large chunks
225g (8oz) boneless venison
 shoulder, cut into large chunks
225g (8oz) boneless rabbit, cut into
 large chunks
1 tsp smoked paprika
pinch of ground allspice
1 tbsp chopped rosemary
1 tbsp Worcestershire sauce
pickles, to serve

Of all the pies in this chapter, it's the hot water crust pastry ones, like this, that I love making the most. If you've never tried this pastry before, now is your moment. There's something very therapeutic about the process – warm, soft and comforting. It's a bit like making your own hug, then filling it with meat! The list of 'game' in the recipe is completely interchangeable, so if you want to use grouse, mallard and quail, then go for it. Equally, if you prefer chicken, lamb and pork, I won't mind.

1 Sift the flour into a bowl and season well.

2 Warm the milk, water and lard in a saucepan until the lard has melted. Bring just to the boil and then pour on to the flour mixture and stir well. Turn out on to a lightly floured surface and knead for 3–4 minutes.

3 Cut the pastry into a third and two-thirds. Roll out the larger piece and press it into a 900g (2lb) loose-bottomed pork pie tin to line it (if the dough is difficult to roll, just press it into the tin). Trim the edge of the dough so it slightly overlaps the rim.

4 Put all the filling ingredients in a large bowl, seasoning with plenty of salt and white pepper, and mix well, then press down into the pastry-lined tin.

5 Brush the beaten egg yolk around the top edge of the pastry. Roll out the smaller piece of pastry into a round to make a lid and place this on top of the pie. Press it down firmly to seal – you can crimp it around the edge if you want it to look fancy. Cut a hole in the centre of the lid, then chill for 20 minutes.

6 Preheat the oven to 180°C/fan 160°C/gas mark 4.

7 Brush the pie with more of the beaten egg yolk, then bake for 1½ hours.

8 I like to leave the pie to cool completely before releasing it from the tin and serving it, but it's also delicious served straight from the oven. Either way, serve it with pickles of your choice.

PORK EMPANADAS

I have a great love of empanadas. They're fundamentally a pasty, but with fire and a crispy pastry. When we were in San Diego we ate some delicious ones – at Cueva Bar on Adams Avenue, if you're ever out there. I like to balance the heat with the cumin, but if you like 'em really fiery, add some raw chilli.

1 Pulse the flour, turmeric, chilli flakes, butter and salt together in a food processor until 'crumby'. Add the milk and egg yolk and pulse until a dough forms.

2 Knead the dough on a lightly floured surface for a few minutes, then cover and chill for at least an hour.

3 Meanwhile, for the filling, heat the oil in a frying or sauté pan and fry the onion, carrot and garlic for about 8 minutes until the vegetables are soft. Add the mince and cook, stirring and breaking it up, until browned. Add the tomato purée, lime rind, cumin and chilli powder and cook for a further 3–4 minutes.

4 Stir in the cubed potato and the beer and bring the mixture to the boil, then simmer for 25 minutes, or until the potato is soft. Leave to cool.

5 Preheat the oven to 200°C/fan 180°C/gas mark 6.

6 Roll out the pastry on a lightly floured surface and cut into 12 circles, each 10cm (4in) in diameter. Place a spoonful of the filling on each pastry circle. Brush the edges with beaten egg, fold over and seal, then mark the sealed edge with the back of a fork.

7 Sit the empanadas on a baking tray and bake for 10 minutes until golden brown.

8 Serve with sweet chilli sauce and/or smoked habanero sauce.

Feeds 4

225g (8oz) plain flour, plus extra for dusting
½ tsp turmeric
½ tsp dried chilli flakes
75g (2¾oz) butter, chilled and cubed
pinch of salt
50ml (2fl oz) milk
1 large egg yolk
beaten egg, to glaze
sweet chilli sauce and/or smoked habanero sauce, to serve

Pork filling

1 tbsp olive oil
1 onion, chopped
1 carrot, diced
1 garlic clove, crushed
225g (8oz) extra-lean minced pork
1 tbsp tomato purée
finely grated rind of 1 lime
¾ tsp ground cumin
1 tsp chilli powder
1 medium potato, cut into 1cm (½in) cubes
100ml (3½fl oz) dark Mexican beer (Negra Modelo) or brown ale/stout
salt and black pepper

BACON & EGG PIE

Feeds 4

butter, for greasing

300g (10½oz) sheet of ready-rolled puff pastry

vegetable oil, for frying

400g (14oz) smoked back bacon lardons

1 red onion, finely sliced

8 large eggs

250ml (9fl oz) double cream

salt and black pepper

1 tbsp chopped parsley

100g (3½oz) Parmesan cheese, grated

ketchup, salad, chips… whatever, to serve

I've recently discovered a love of quiche… I know, it's not very manly, is it? (Or at least not according to Bruce Feirstein's 1982 classic tribute to masculinity, *Real Men Don't Eat Quiche*.) But that combination of pastry, egg and whatever else you fancy is very appealing. This beauty is a popular staff meal at EARLE. It feels and looks more manly than a regular quiche – I'm thinking more cowboys on the range with smoky barbecue beans around a campfire… or perhaps it's actually more *Brokeback Mountain* than *Bonanza*? Either way, it's a doddle to make, tasty as anything and leaves all men enough time to moisturize and preen before tea.

1 Preheat the oven to 180°C/fan 160°C/gas mark 4.

2 Grease a baking dish, approximately 30cm x 25cm (12in x 10in), line the dish with the pastry and trim the edges, then prick the base all over with a fork.

3 Heat a little oil in a frying or sauté pan and fry the bacon lardons until crisp. Remove from the pan and leave to cool a little.

4 Add a bit more oil to the pan and fry the onion for about 5 minutes until soft.

5 Beat the eggs, cream and seasoning together in a large bowl, then spoon in the bacon lardons, onion and parsley.

6 Pour the egg mixture into the pastry-lined dish and top with the Parmesan. Bake for about 45 minutes until the filling is puffed up and lightly browned.

7 Leave the pie to cool a little, then serve with whatever you fancy.

Feeds 4–6

300g (10½oz) ready-made shortcrust pastry

15g (½oz) butter, plus extra for greasing

½ onion, finely chopped

100g (3½oz) chestnut mushrooms, trimmed and sliced

250g (9oz) cooked chicken, shredded

1 carrot, diced

1 tbsp fresh or frozen peas

1 tbsp plain flour, plus extra for dusting

100ml (3½fl oz) red wine

100ml (3½fl oz) chicken stock

beaten egg, to glaze

potatoes and vegetables, to serve

CHICKEN PIE

Next time you have a dinner party, why not make this fabulous chicken plate pie? Just watch your guests' faces light up as you bring this big old Desperate Dan of a pie to the table and let them all tuck in. I predict that the conversation will happily move away from property, schools and red wine into the more interesting realms of who's better, Peter Griffin or Cartman. If that makes no sense to you, you should defo make this pie at once.

1 Cut the pastry in half and roll it out on a lightly floured surface into 2 circles big enough to line and top a 23–25cm (9–10in) pie plate. Grease the pie plate, then sit one of the circles on it.

2 For the filling, melt the butter in a frying or sauté pan and fry the onion and mushies for about 8 minutes until soft. Add the chicken, carrot and peas and cook for a further 2–3 minutes.

3 Sprinkle on the flour and cook, stirring, for 2 minutes. Stir in the wine and stock and simmer for 25 minutes until the mixture is thick and glossy. Leave to cool a little.

4 Preheat the oven to 200°C/fan 180°C/gas mark 6.

5 Spoon the mixture on to the pastry base, leaving a good 2.5cm (1in) border all round. Top with the other pastry circle and press around the edge with the back of a fork to seal. Brush with the beaten egg.

6 Bake for 30 minutes until golden brown. Serve with spuds and veg.

CHICKEN BALTI PASTY

Makes 6 pasties

225g (8oz) plain flour, plus extra
   for dusting
75g (2¾oz) butter, chilled and cubed
pinch of salt
50ml (2fl oz) milk
1 large egg yolk
beaten egg, to glaze
pickle, to serve

Chicken balti filling

vegetable oil, for frying
2 skinless chicken breasts, about 200g
   (7oz) each, cut into bite-sized chunks
3 onions, sliced
2 garlic cloves, crushed
2 chillies (red or green), chopped
3cm (1¼in) piece of fresh root
   ginger, peeled and grated
1 tsp turmeric
1 tsp ground cumin
1 tsp ground coriander
1 tsp paprika
1 tsp garam masala
pinch of ground cinnamon
1 tbsp tomato purée
1 red pepper, cored, deseeded and cut
   into small squares
75ml (2½fl oz) passata
salt and black pepper
handful of coriander leaves

One of my many guilty pleasures is the humble pasty. And it's not just the delicious, traditional ones, but also the high street, motorway service station and pub ones that I know I should resist. The joy of pastry and filling can't be beaten, and I also love the new fillings of chicken tikka and Mexican chilli. And then, for my own and your delectation, this bad boy came up with chicken balti. I feel guilty already…

1 Pulse the flour, butter and salt together in a food processor until 'crumby'. Add the milk and egg yolk and pulse until a dough forms. Knead the dough on a lightly floured surface for a few minutes, then cover and chill for at least an hour.

2 For the filling, heat a little oil in a frying or sauté pan and fry the chicken until browned all over. Remove from the pan.

3 Add a bit more oil to the pan and fry the onions, garlic, chillies and ginger for 5 minutes. Return the chicken to the pan, add the spices and cook for 5 minutes, then stir in the tomato purée and cook for 5 minutes to remove the bitterness.

4 Add the red pepper and passata and simmer for 20 minutes (you may need to add a little water or stock to stop the mixture drying out). Season and stir in the coriander leaves, then leave to cool completely.

5 Preheat the oven to 200°C/fan 180°C/gas mark 6.

6 Divide the pastry into 6, then roll out each piece on a lightly floured surface and cut out 6 x 23cm (9in) circles. Divide the filling between the pastry circles, then brush the edges with beaten egg. Bring up either side of each circle to meet in the centre and pinch together to seal and make your dinosaur back edge.

7 Sit the pasties on a baking tray and bake for 25–30 minutes until golden brown. Serve with your fave pickle.

THAI-SPICED FISH PIE

This recipe is something I've played around with for a while. When I have a night off I often cook it for Ali, Flo and Hamish, and it's always a tremendous success. What you get is a mild Thai spice (but up it to extreme if you fancy), a creamy coconut sauce and a half spud, half sweet spud topping. I am made up with it, and I hope you like it too.

1 Preheat the oven to 200°C/fan 180°C/gas mark 6.

2 Heat a little oil in a large saucepan and gently fry the onion or shallots, garlic, lemon grass and chilli for 3–4 minutes until softened. Add the coconut milk, milk and lime leaves and bring to the boil, then turn down to a bare simmer.

3 Pop the fish and prawns into the pan and poach for 6 minutes, then remove and transfer to a 23cm (9in) square baking dish, setting the poaching liquor aside.

4 Melt the butter in a medium saucepan, add the flour and cook, stirring, for 1 minute until a roux (smooth paste) forms. Gradually add the poaching liquor, stirring constantly to keep the mixture smooth, then add the lime rind and juice. Bring to the boil, then simmer for 5 minutes, stirring all the time. Season well.

5 Stir the peas and coriander into the sauce, then pour it over the fish.

6 Mash the cooked spud and sweet spuds with the butter and spring onions, season well and spread over the fish. Make pretty patterns in the topping with the back of a fork.

7 Bake for 25 minutes, then finish it off under a hot grill to crisp up the topping. Serve with stir-fried Asian greens.

Serves 6

vegetable oil, for frying

1 onion or 2 banana shallots, finely chopped

1 garlic clove, crushed

1 lemon grass stalk, very finely chopped

1 green chilli, finely chopped

400ml can coconut milk

100ml (3½fl oz) milk

2 kaffir lime leaves, shredded

400g (14oz) monkfish tail, trimmed

200g (7oz) skinless salmon fillet

200g (7oz) uncooked peeled king prawns

50g (1¾oz) butter

50g (1¾oz) plain flour

finely grated rind and juice of 1 lime

salt and black pepper

100g (3½oz) fresh or frozen peas

handful of chopped coriander

500g (1lb 2oz) potato, boiled and drained

250g (9oz) sweet potato, boiled and drained

200g (7oz) butter

2 spring onions, chopped

stir-fried Asian greens, to serve

TIM
HATES
CORIANDER

One of the first 'campaigns' that I got embroiled in on *Something for the Weekend* was the great coriander debate. **Tim announced that he hated it and that it tasted of soap**, while for me it's one of the best herbs around. For the next three months, wherever either of us went, people would express their thoughts on this pressing problem. Not only that, we also discovered that there are websites for equally strange people like Tim who can't stand the stuff. So for all of you, UNLUCKY! Here's a chapter full of recipes packed full of coriander.

A SELECTION OF PAKORA WITH CORIANDER YOGURT

Feeds 6

vegetable oil, for frying and
  deep-frying
6 onions, sliced
2 garlic cloves, crushed
1 (or 2) red chillies, finely chopped
1 skinless chicken breast, about 200g
  (7oz), cooked and cut into strips
24 uncooked peeled baby prawns or
  12 uncooked peeled king prawns

Batter

450g (1lb) gram flour, seasoned
  with salt and black pepper
about 250ml (9fl oz) warm water

Coriander yogurt

1 bunch of coriander
75ml (2½fl oz) rice vinegar
salt
250ml (9fl oz) natural yogurt

The joy of a crispy onion bhaji is one of my favourite taste sensations. That crunch of batter, the sweet onion and then the kick of a little bit of chilli is divine. This recipe gives you a trio of pakoras – classic onion, prawn and chicken. The addition of the lovely acidic, vinegary yogurt sauce makes for a taste of heaven.

1 Heat a glug of oil in a large frying or sauté pan and gently fry the onions, garlic and chilli for about 15 minutes until they begin to caramelize. Leave to cool slightly.

2 For the batter, put the seasoned flour into a bowl, make a well in the centre and gradually add the water, whisking it into the flour. Do this by eye, as you need to make sure the consistency is of thick double cream, so you may need more or less water than specified.

3 Divide the onion mixture between 3 separate bowls. Leaving one plain, add the chicken to another bowl and prawns to the remaining one (if you're using the king prawns, cut them up a bit first).

4 Now divide the batter between the 3 bowls and mix well. Half-fill a deep-fat fryer or deep, heavy-based saucepan with vegetable oil and heat to 180°C, or until a small cube of bread tossed into the oil turns golden in about 30 seconds. Starting with the plain onion mixture, deep-fry, in batches, by lifting tablespoonfuls of the mixture and dropping them individually into the oil. Fry each batch for about 4–6 minutes until crisp and golden, then remove with a slotted spoon and drain on kitchen paper.

5 Meanwhile, for the coriander yogurt, in a food processor, blend the coriander, vinegar and a little salt together until smooth, then add the yogurt and blend briefly to combine.

6 Serve one each of the pakoras with some of the yogurt for dipping.

CORIANDER & CORNBREAD MUFFINS

Makes 12–16

225g (8oz) polenta

225g (8oz) plain flour

1 tbsp baking powder

50g (1¾oz) caster sugar

1 tsp celery salt

225ml (8fl oz) buttermilk, soured
    cream or yogurt

75ml (2½fl oz) vegetable oil

75g (2¾oz) drained canned
    sweetcorn kernels

1 egg

½ bunch of coriander, chopped

1 tbsp chopped chives

I used to find the texture of polenta (cornmeal) a bit off-putting – too gritty for me. But a few years ago we were on holiday in California and ate at a great Mexican restaurant in San Diego called El Comal. Amongst many delicious treats (green mole being a highlight) was a cornbread muffin, stuffed with a spicy prawn salad, and suddenly the texture of the muffin made sense with that of the food. So I recommend you eat these fellas, either warm and buttered or with a big bowl of chilli or spicy Mexican fish soup – or with my Lamb and Coriander Stew (see page 62).

1 Preheat the oven to 180°C/fan 160°C/gas mark 4. Line 1–2 muffin trays with paper muffin cases – the mixture should make 12–16 muffins.

2 Mix all the dry ingredients together in a large bowl.

3 In a separate bowl, whisk all the remaining wet ingredients together.

4 Mix the wet mixture into the dry one, but until only just combined – don't overwork.

5 Spoon the mixture into the muffin cases, then bake for 15–20 minutes until risen and golden brown. Serve with pride.

GOAN GREEN CHICKEN CURRY

Feeds 6

3 skinless chicken breasts, about 200g (7oz) each, cut into big chunks

200g (7oz) potatoes, cut into 3cm (1¼in) cubes, blanched in salted boiling water for 2 minutes and drained

1 tbsp fresh or frozen peas, or topped and tailed fine green beans

lime wedges, to garnish

boiled rice and naan bread, to serve

Curry paste

1 onion, roughly chopped

4 green bird's eye chillies

1 garlic clove, peeled

1 tbsp caster sugar

2 tsp tamarind pulp, thinned with a little hot water and then rubbed to form a loose paste

1 tsp ground coriander

2 tbsp vegetable oil

Green sauce

400g (14oz) spinach leaves

1 bunch of fresh coriander, plus extra to garnish

good handful of mint

400ml can coconut milk

salt

There's a very unassuming curry house on Westbourne Grove in London called the Star of Bengal, but don't be fooled by its simple appearance, because the food is excellent, particularly the Goan green chicken curry. It's such a delicious mix of my favourite flavours – mint, spinach and, of course, coriander. It manages to taste both fresh and slow-roasted at the same time. So after a few visits I asked for the secret… of course, they wouldn't tell me! But this feels about right – let me know what you think.

1 For the curry paste, in a food processor, blend the onion, chillies, garlic, sugar, tamarind and ground coriander to a fine paste.

2 Heat the oil in a saucepan and gently fry the curry paste for about 4–5 minutes until it releases its fragrance.

3 For the sauce, blend the spinach, coriander, mint and coconut milk together in the processor (you don't need to wash it between uses), add to the paste pan and bring to the boil. Simmer for 5 minutes – you may need to add a little water or stock to thin it down – then season with salt.

4 Add the chicken to the sauce and simmer for 20 minutes until cooked through, adding the blanched spuds about 10 minutes in and cooking them until tender, and then the veggies for the final 5 minutes.

5 Garnish with more coriander and with lime wedges, and serve with boiled rice and naan bread.

LAMB & CORIANDER STEW

The fragrant, perfumed quality of coriander is what I love best. This has a great big powerful nose on it – a whiff of this stew and I'm in heaven. Once your nostrils have had a treat, then your taste buds are in for the time of their lives. If this dish was a girl, you wouldn't take her home to meet your mum, if you get my drift.

1 Heat a little oil in a flameproof casserole dish and fry the lamb until browned and sealed on all sides. Remove from the pan.

2 Add a bit more oil to the pan and fry the onion, garlic and chilli for about 5 minutes until softened. Put the lamb back in the pan, add the squash and ground spices and cook gently for 5 minutes.

3 Add the tomatoes and stock and bring to boil. Stir in half the coriander, then simmer for about 1½ hours.

4 Add the rosewater, chickpeas and lemon rind and juice and cook for 5 minutes more. Stir in the rest of the coriander, season and serve – take the whole dish to the table with the lid on, then remove the lid to get the full effect. This is great accompanied by something starchy and served with natural yogurt.

Feeds 4–6

olive oil, for frying

450g (1lb) boneless lamb shoulder, cut into decent-sized chunks

1 onion, chopped

2 garlic cloves, sliced

1 red chilli, chopped

200g (7oz) peeled and deseeded butternut squash, cut into 2.5cm (1in) cubes

1 tbsp ground sumac

1 tbsp ground coriander

1 tbsp ground cinnamon

400g can chopped tomatoes

200ml (7fl oz) lamb stock

2 big bunches of fresh coriander, well chopped

1 tbsp rosewater

400g can chickpeas, drained and rinsed

finely grated rind and juice of 1 lemon

salt and black pepper

rice, couscous, bulgur wheat, spuds or flatbread and natural yogurt, to serve

WILD BOAR & CORIANDER BURGERS WITH SWEET ROASTED PEPPERS

Feeds 6

4 red peppers

vegetable oil, for rubbing and brushing

100ml (3½fl oz) red wine vinegar

100g (3½oz) demerara sugar

2 tsp smoked paprika

6 fancy burger buns – ciabatta, sourdough or whatever is trendy in breadland

The burgers

800g (1lb 12oz) minced wild boar

200g (7oz) minced pork

1 bunch of coriander, finely chopped

1 tbsp ground fennel seeds

salt and black pepper

The trimmings

mayo

gherkins

tomato

lettuce… oh and chips!

My very good friend Peter Gott keeps the most magnificent wild boars in Cumbria at Sillfield Farm. The meat is divine and a trip to the farm is one of the kids' best days out (Peter is also as mad as cheese, I might add). So while I'm using boar in this recipe because I love it with coriander, it will do with beef, pork or lamb.

1 Preheat the oven to 200°C/fan 180°C/gas mark 6.

2 Rub a little oil over the red peppers, then roast them on a baking tray for about 15 minutes until their skins have blackened. Remove the peppers from the oven and put them in a sealable plastic bag. Seal the bag and leave the peppers to cool, then skin and deseed them and cut them into strips.

3 Boil the vinegar and sugar in a saucepan for 3–4 minutes until the sugar has melted and the mixture becomes syrupy. Stir in the paprika and peppers, then leave to cool.

4 Now for the burgers… dead easy. Ignore recipes adding egg and breadcrumbs – all you need is meat and seasoning. So, with your hands, mix the minced meats, coriander, fennel and salt and pepper together really well, then mould into 6 burgers. Chill for 20 minutes.

5 Brush the burgers on both sides with oil and cook in a hot griddle pan or frying pan or under a hot grill for about 6 minutes on each side until cooked through.

6 Slip a burger into each bun, top with the sweet roasted peppers and serve with all the trimmings.

I LIKE PRAWNS BUT THEY DON'T LIKE ME

There are some expressions that have long since been in your vocabulary, but you don't always realize how funny they are. I've often heard variations on the title of this chapter, but it really made me laugh one night at EARLE. I was chatting to a lovely lady customer who wanted everything 'plain' – a simple piece of grilled fish or meat with plain veg, which was fine. We were chatting away as I got the dish together, which was a piece of sole, and I asked her if she'd like some prawns with it, and she replied, **'I like prawns, but they don't like me'**. Cue lots of fishies on their dishies. I also put the lady in touch with a good therapist and now her persecution complex about crustacea has gone and she's befriended a couple of tiger prawns.

STUFFED LEMON SOLE

Every now and again my grandparents (dad's side; Italian mum) would take us to a brilliant place in Birkenhead called the Bowler Hat. It had that old-school charm of waiters who were at least a million years old but great at their job, proper metal domes to cover the food and keep it warm, and an air of friendly stuffiness. It was also the first place I saw such delights as stuffed trout, whitebait – and this yummy stuffed lemon sole. Far too grand for a little kid like me, but somehow, I think, a starting point for my love of food and restaurants.

Feeds 4

75g (2¾oz) butter

2 fennel bulbs, trimmed and finely chopped

3 garlic cloves, sliced

24 pitted green olives, chopped

300g (10½oz) uncooked peeled baby prawns

juice of 1 lemon

1 tbsp chopped tarragon

salt and black pepper

4 small whole lemon soles, cleaned

olive oil, for drizzling

simple boiled, buttered new potatoes and green beans, to serve

1 Melt the butter in a frying or sauté pan and gently fry the fennel, garlic and olives for about 8 minutes until the fennel is soft.

2 Add the prawns, lemon juice and tarragon, season and cook for 3–4 minutes, or until the prawns are cooked through.

3 Preheat the oven to 200°C/fan 180°C/gas mark 6.

4 Using a sharp flexible knife, make a cut down the centre back of each fish, then cut along the bone either side of the central cut to form a pocket. Push the prawn mixture into the pockets, lay the fish on a baking tray and drizzle with a little oil.

5 Bake for about 8 minutes until just cooked through, then serve with simple boiled potatoes and green beans.

JERK
SNAPPER WITH RICE 'N' PEAS

I sat on the harbour in Antigua and ate a plate of this about a year ago. The day was hot and muggy, and I was tired after trailing around a food market sampling tamarind sweets, bread fruit and pure cocoa, and drinking from fresh, young coconuts. So we wandered over to a shack near the harbour and ordered the rice 'n' peas and snapper. It came on paper plates and smelt divine. I splashed some proper hot sauce on top and squeezed over a bit of lime, then threw off my flip flops, ordered a beer and kicked back, savouring the moment. After I'd finished, I chatted to the guy who'd been cooking and asked him for his jerk seasoning recipe. What you have below will feed a good few people. Just add enough oil to combine, then you're done.

1 For the jerk seasoning, simply place all the ingredients in a screw-top jar and seal with the lid. It will keep in a cool place for a good couple of weeks.

2 For the rice 'n' peas, heat the oil in a saucepan and fry the onion for about 5 minutes until soft but not coloured.

3 Add the rice and stir well, then stir in the stock and coconut milk. Bring to the boil and add the beans and thyme, then cover and simmer for about 20 minutes until the rice is cooked. Season well.

4 Meanwhile, rub 50g (1¾oz) of the jerk seasoning into the snapper fillets. Heat a little oil in a frying or sauté pan and fry the fish over a medium heat for 2 minutes on each side until golden brown and just cooked through. Garnish with coriander and serve with the rice 'n' peas, hot sauce and cold beer.

Feeds 4

4 red snapper fillets, 150g (5½oz) each
vegetable oil, for frying
coriander leaves, to garnish
hot sauce and cold beer, to serve

Jerk seasoning

2 tbsp dried onions
2 tbsp dried thyme
1 tbsp ground allspice
1 tsp thyme leaves
½ tsp ground cinnamon
½ tsp cayenne pepper
½ tsp paprika
salt and black pepper
2 tbsp vegetable oil

Rice 'n' peas

50ml (2fl oz) vegetable oil
1 onion, finely chopped
300g (10½oz) white long-grain rice
400ml (14fl oz) chicken stock
400ml can coconut milk
400g can kidney beans, drained and rinsed
3 tbsp thyme leaves
salt and black pepper

HALIBUT WRAPPED IN BREAD ON CAULI PURÉE

Feeds 4

8 slices of white bread, crusts removed
200g (7oz) clarified butter
4 halibut fillets, about 150g (5½oz) each
salt and black pepper
coriander leaves, to garnish

Cauli purée
1 tbsp olive oil
½ onion, chopped
250g (9oz) cauliflower florets
2 tsp curry powder
75ml (2½fl oz) white wine
200ml (7fl oz) double cream
salt and black pepper
1 tbsp capers

I've been very lucky to be a judge for the army on a good few catering competitions, my favourite being the Rhino Caterer in Germany, where I competed in the 'improvised' event. This is where you make your own ovens from old filing cabinets, boxes and the like, and hobs from sheets of metal and fire, then have to create gourmet food out of a random bag of ingredients. This is a dish that worked brilliantly (although it was with haddock, not halibut). The effect of rolling out the bread to make a dough is superb, as it crisps it and gives a great texture to the fish, and then the mild spice of the purée cut with vinegary capers is a winner. I got a gold medal and a trophy, in case you're wondering.

1 Roll the bread slices with a rolling pin to make them as flat and squashed as you can. Lay out the bread, overlapping 4 pairs of slices to make 4 bready rectangles just a little wider than the fish. Brush the bread with some of the clarified butter.

2 Now brush the fish with some of the butter and season well, then place a fillet on each bready rectangle and wrap the bread around each fillet to form 4 parcels. Chill for 30 minutes to stiffen up.

3 For the cauli purée, heat the oil in a saucepan and fry the onion for about 5 minutes until softened. Add the cauli and cook for 7–8 minutes until tender.

4 Add the curry powder and cook, stirring, for a couple of minutes, then add the wine and simmer until reduced by half. Stir in the cream and simmer for 5 minutes more. Season well, then fold in the capers.

5 Meanwhile, brush the chilled fish parcels with the rest of the clarified butter. Fry in a large hot frying pan for 3 minutes on each side until crisp and golden.

6 Drain on kitchen paper and serve on top of the purée, garnished with coriander leaves.

HAZELNUT-CRUSTED HALIBUT WITH CREAMY LENTILS

Feeds 6

100g (3½oz) granary or similar breadcrumbs

100g (3½oz) roasted hazelnuts, chopped

1 tbsp chopped tarragon

100g (3½oz) butter, cubed

salt and black pepper

6 halibut steaks, about 175g (6oz) each

vegetable oil, for rubbing

Creamy lentils

olive oil, for frying

1 red onion, finely diced

1 red pepper, cored, deseeded and finely diced

1 garlic clove, crushed

500g (1lb 2oz) cooked Puy lentils

100ml (3½fl oz) white wine

juice of 2 lemons

350ml (½ pint) double cream, plus extra if needed

150g (5½oz) baby spinach, finely shredded

1 tbsp chopped mint

1 tbsp chopped tarragon

salt and black pepper

One of the great things about having mates for a long time is that they never cease to amaze you. One day in the pub – the recently demised Picture House in Liverpool – and after a Liverpool game, we were chatting about various things and someone came to the table with a bag of salted peanuts. From this point we somehow got into a deep, heated exchange about 'your favourite nut' (seriously). Now, at the time I fought long and hard for the classic macadamia – sweet, buttery, tasty. But with hindsight, I think the hazelnut is my fave, being great in dressings, sauces, salads and as a crumb, as in this instance – and that's before I've started on Nutella, hazelnut lattes and choccy bars. Oh, the winning nut? Cashew. Go figure!

1 For the lentils, heat some oil in a saucepan and fry the onion, red pepper and garlic for 5 minutes until soft.

2 Add the lentils, stir well and warm through for 2–3 minutes. Add the wine, crank up the heat and cook until reduced by two-thirds.

3 Add the lemon juice and cook to reduce some more, then stir in the cream and spinach and cook for 3–5 minutes until reduced to a thick sauce (if the mixture reduces too quickly, add a little more cream or even a splash of water). Finally, stir in the herbs and season.

4 Meanwhile, preheat the oven to 200°C/fan 180°C/gas mark 6.

5 Make the topping by rubbing together the breadcrumbs, hazelnuts, tarragon and butter with your fingertips, and seasoning well (it doesn't matter if it 'clumps' when it cooks – it'll be superb).

6 Rub the fish steaks with oil. Cook in a hot frying pan for about 1 minute on each side to seal, then remove and transfer to a baking tray.

7 Press the topping on to each piece of yummy halibut, then bake for about 8–10 minutes until the topping is lightly browned and the fish is cooked through. Serve on top of the lentils.

BEETROOT-CURED SALMON

I love curing, brining, preserving and pickling, and this incredible cured salmon dish always looks stunning as the fish has a lovely, rich, pinky-purple edge. It tastes superb, too, as the sugar, salt and beets add an earthy quality to the fish. It also looks like it's really hard to do, but it isn't at all – it's a doddle. Just mix, rub, leave, wash, slice and eat.

1 For the curing mix, in a food processor, purée the beets with the sugar, salt, honey and fennel seeds until smooth.

2 Place the salmon in a large baking dish, spread the curing mix over it and press it in well. Cover and chill for at least 24 hours.

3 The next day, rinse the curing mix carefully off the salmon and pat it dry. Slice the fish into thin pieces.

4 For the horseradish cream, mix all the ingredients together in a bowl.

5 Place about 3–5 slices of the salmon on each plate. Accompany with a dollop of the horseradish cream and serve with sliced cornichons and pumpernickel bread.

Feeds 6–8

about 500–700g (1lb 2oz–1lb 9oz) side of salmon, trimmed of fat

Curing mix

8 raw beetroots, peeled and roughly chopped

750g (1lb 10oz) caster sugar

500g (1lb 2oz) coarse sea salt

50ml (2fl oz) clear honey

1 tbsp fennel seeds

Horseradish cream

200ml (7fl oz) lightly whipped cream

50ml (2fl oz) soured cream

100g (3½oz) finely grated fresh horseradish

juice of 1 lemon

salt and black pepper

To serve

sliced cornichons

finely sliced pumpernickel bread

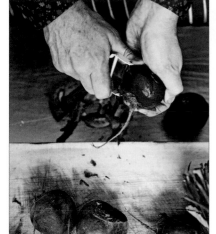

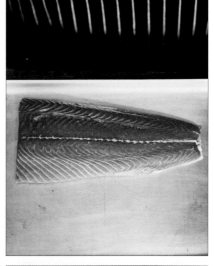

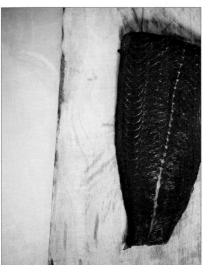

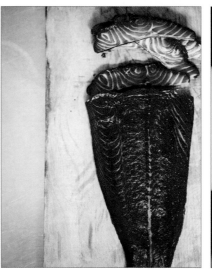

COD WITH SEAFOOD RISOTTO

Remember Batchelors Savoury Rice? I used to love that, with its heady mix of herbs and spices and a touch of seasoning, as the ad went. I had a real thing for a plate of savoury rice – with fish fingers on top and a good dollop of tom sauce, I was in 10-year-old heaven! Anyway, the purpose of this ramble is that my fave meal as a boy is the inspiration for this dish. I still love rice and fish – kedgeree, fish tikka and rice, and so on – and this beauty is full of flavour, and almost as good as Mr Batchelor's efforts.

Feeds 4

vegetable oil, for rubbing
4 skin-on cod fillets, about 175g (6oz) each
salt and black pepper
knob of butter
squeeze of lemon juice

Seafood risotto

15g (½oz) butter
1 tbsp olive oil
1 onion, finely sliced
1 garlic clove, crushed
400g (14oz) Arborio rice
glug of white wine
about 800ml (scant 1½ pints) chicken stock, kept warm in a saucepan
about 500g (1lb 2oz) assorted shellfish and fish – uncooked shell-on prawns, live mussels in shells (scrubbed and 'beards' removed), skinless salmon fillet etc
100g (3½oz) peas (frozen are fine)
8 tomatoes, skinned and chopped
salt and black pepper
handful of chopped tarragon

1 For the risotto, melt the butter with the olive oil in a saucepan and fry the onion and garlic for about 5 minutes until soft.

2 Add the rice and stir well, making sure every grain is coated, then add the wine and bubble until reduced to nearly nothing. Take a close look at the rice – the husks should be translucent and appear to have hairline cracks on them (this is known as 'cracking' and means that the rice is ready for the liquid). Add a good ladleful of the warm stock, stir well and cook the rice over a medium heat, continuing to stir occasionally, until nearly all the stock is absorbed. Repeat until you've added all but a final ladleful of the stock and the rice is cooked but still a touch 'al dente'.

3 Add the mixed shellfish and fish (if using mussels, bin any that are open and fail to close when tapped against the side of the sink), peas and toms with the rest of the stock and stir well. Cook for 4–5 minutes until the shellfish and fish are cooked (chuck any mussels that haven't opened) and the stock is absorbed. Season and stir in the tarragon.

4 Meanwhile, rub oil on to the cod fillets, season and then cook, skin-side down, in a fairly hot frying pan for 4–5 minutes to crisp the skin.

5 Flip the fish over and cook for another 4–5 minutes, then turn back on to the skin side. Add the butter to the pan and baste the fish, then squeeze over the lemon juice.

6 Drain the cod on kitchen paper, then serve on top of the risotto.

POTTED BROWN SHRIMPS & CRAB WITH LEMON BEANS

One of my favourite treats as a kid was going to Parkgate, on the posh, south side of the Wirral in Cheshire. There we'd get the best ice cream (combo of lime 'n' lemon with a scoop of strawberry, my fave) from Nicholls, go to the swings, then walk back on to the front. Parkgate had been a massive port, but as the Dee Estuary silted up it declined, and now the vegetation is up to the sea wall and the sea is just a distant memory. But there's still a small number of brown shrimps there, and as a kid (as now) it was the treat of all treats to eat 'em warm out of a bag. So this recipe uses the shrimps with crab, and there's a fresh bean salad with a lemony dressing to eat with it.

1 Put the shellfish, spices, seasoning, lemon juice and the softened butter in a bowl and mix well, but gently.

2 Divide the mixture between 4 individual ramekins and press down, then pour over the melted butter. Chill until set and ready to serve.

3 Whisk all the dressing ingredients together in a bowl.

4 For the salad, chop the herbs, then mix with the beans and celery in a separate bowl and season. Pour over the dressing and gently toss to combine. Serve with the potted crab and buttered brown bread.

Feeds 4

115g (4oz) cooked white crabmeat
75g (2¾oz) cooked peeled brown shrimps
pinch of cayenne pepper
freshly grated nutmeg, to taste
salt and black pepper
juice of ½ lemon
100g (3½oz) softened butter, plus 50g (1¾oz) melted butter
buttered brown bread, to serve

Lemon dressing

150ml (¼ pint) extra virgin olive oil
finely grated rind and juice of 2 lemons
1 tbsp Dijon mustard
1 tbsp white wine vinegar
salt and black pepper

Bean salad

handful of parsley
handful of coriander
400g can butter beans, drained and rinsed
1 celery stick, very finely chopped
salt and black pepper

PRAWN CUSTARDS
WITH FRENCH TOAST

I dream of these, they're so delicious – a savoury, oriental-spiced ramekin full of loveliness. These also work with soaked, dried shiitake mushrooms, but for me the prawns make it… and the French toast. Is this fusion food, then?

1 Toss the prawns in the soy and sugar in a non-metallic bowl, then cover and leave to marinate in the fridge for at least 10 minutes.

2 Preheat the oven to 170°C/fan 150°C/gas mark 3½.

3 Beat the eggs in a bowl. Meanwhile, bring the milk, cream and dashi to a simmer, then take off the heat and pour over eggs. Beat well and add the sherry, then strain through a fine sieve.

4 Put one prawn in the bottom of each of 4 individual ramekins and pour over the custard. Stand the ramekins in a roasting tin, fill halfway up their sides with water and cover with foil. Bake for about 30 minutes until the custard has set.

5 Meanwhile, for the French toast, beat the eggs, milk, sugar and spices together in a bowl. Soak the bread in the mixture until well coated.

6 Melt the butter in a frying pan, add the bread, in batches, and cook over a medium heat for about 2 minutes on each side until crisp.

7 Sprinkle sesame seeds over the custards to garnish and eat with the French toast.

Feeds 4

8 cooked peeled king prawns
3 tbsp Japanese soy sauce
1 tbsp caster sugar
4 large eggs
200ml (7fl oz) milk
200ml (7fl oz) double cream
200ml (7fl oz) dashi
splash of sherry
sesame seeds, to garnish

French toast
2 large eggs
100ml (3½fl oz) milk
pinch of caster sugar
pinch of freshly grated nutmeg
pinch of cayenne pepper
4 slices of bread, cut diagonally in half
  to make triangles
50g (1¾oz) butter

77

Feeds 4–6

150g (5½oz) butter
225ml (8fl oz) water
225g (8oz) plain flour
6 large eggs
pinch of salt

Lobster and smoked salmon filling

250g (9oz) light cream cheese
100g (3½oz) smoked salmon slices, chopped
pinch of dried chilli flakes
finely grated rind and juice of 1 lime
salt and black pepper
1 tbsp chopped dill
150g (5½oz) cooked lobster meat
butter, for frying lobster (optional)

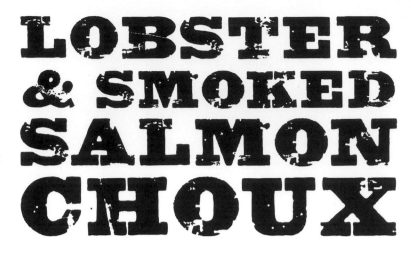

LOBSTER & SMOKED SALMON CHOUX

Choux buns, éclairs, *croque en bouche*, Paris-Brest… all delicious variations on the same thing: crisp, tasty choux pastry. Now I love, as in this recipe, to use choux pastry as a savoury ingredient. This is a proper 'eat like a celebrity' dish in which you make the choux buns smaller rather than bigger so that you can pop the whole bun into your mouth in one go. They're great for parties, great as a starter and great as a posh snack if you're trying to impress someone.

1 Preheat the oven to 200°C/fan 180°C/gas mark 6. Line a baking tray with greaseproof paper.

2 Put the butter and water in a saucepan and heat until the butter melts and water comes to the boil. Take the pan off the heat, tip in all the flour at once and beat well with a wooden spoon until smooth and the mixture leaves the side of the pan.

3 Beat in the eggs, one at a time, with the spoon (it's pretty tough on the old arms this one), then add salt.

4 Transfer the mixture to a piping bag and leave it to cool for a few minutes. Now pipe 'blobs' – balls of about 2.5cm (1in) – on to the lined baking tray. Bake for about 25–30 minutes. You want the buns to be golden and firm, and the aim is get them to dry out

in the middle, so I quite often put them on the bottom shelf to bake for another 5–10 minutes after the initial baking time, to make sure they're right.

5 When they are ready, take the buns out of the oven and let them cool on a wire rack before slicing across the middle ready to take the filling.

6 To make the filling, beat the cheese, salmon, chilli flakes and lime rind and juice together in a bowl and season well. Spread over the bottom halves of the choux buns, then lay the lobster meat on top (you can if you like quickly fry the lobster in butter beforehand to warm it) and sprinkle over the dill. Sit the tops on the buns, and then serve.

Bacon butty, juicy cheese burger, 28 day aged rib eye steak, corn fed duck breast, pork chop, crackling, chicken tikka, slow roasted lamb shank, chorizo in sherry, thick cut ham, Serrano ham, salami… see what happens when you start making a list of meaty favourites in your head? Whenever I'm poorly (usually with man flu) I crave a roast dinner, succulent meat with lots of veg and a cracking gravy. When I feel like celebrating I feel like a rib eye from Frosty the Butcher with chips and béarnaise, when it's Tuesday I want corned beef with pickle on my butty, when I'm cooking for (and with) the kids it's meatballs all the way. Now I've written this info I need to get the pan on and cook some bacon, just in the interests of research you understand!

ROAST FORE RIB OF BEEF WITH DAUPHINOISE

Is there a dish more satisfying than a tasty roast rib of beef? This is my guide to getting it right. First, make sure you buy a good-quality piece of beef – the fore rib is on the bone and so full of flavour. You want a short-bone rib, preferably aged for at least 21 days. There should be a layer of white fat with a hint of yellow over the meat, and within the meat lovely creamy white marbling. The fat will give flavour and moisture, with the marbling 'melting' during cooking. If you can, make a few incisions in the fat and rub in salt and black pepper, and rub seasoning over the bones too. Cover and stick it in the fridge until the next day. If you don't have time to do that, then leave it for at least 4 hours before cooking.

Feeds 4

2 fore ribs of beef, about 700–800g (1lb 9oz–1lb 12oz), each rubbed with salt and black pepper

vegetables of your choice, to serve (optional)

Potatoes dauphinoise

25g (1oz) butter, plus extra for greasing

1 onion, finely sliced

1 garlic clove, crushed

800g (1lb 12oz) potatoes, finely sliced

salt and black pepper

285ml carton double cream

285ml carton single cream

200g (7oz) Parmesan cheese, finely grated

Gravy

2 tbsp plain flour

about 300ml (½ pint) red wine

salt

about 300ml (½ pint) beef stock

few sprigs of rosemary

1 For the spuds, grease a baking dish about 25cm x 15cm (10in x 6in). Melt the butter in a small frying pan and fry the onion and garlic until softened but not browned. Then simply layer up the spuds and onion in the buttered dish, seasoning each layer.

2 Combine the creams and season well, then pour over the spuds and onion and leave to stand for about 20 minutes. Meanwhile, preheat the oven to 180°C/fan 160°C/gas mark 4.

3 Scatter the Parmesan over the spud mixture and bake for about 1½ hours until the potatoes are tender and the topping is well browned.

4 While the spuds are baking, and once you've seasoned and rested the beef (see above), add the fore ribs, in batches, to a hot frying pan and cook until sealed on all sides, making sure there's a lovely colour all over. Transfer to a large roasting tray and roast for 45–50 minutes. Leave to rest in a warm place for at least 20 minutes before removing from the roasting tray and carving into big, thick slices.

5 For the gravy, tip away all the fat from the roasting tray except for about a tablespoonful. Heat this in the tray on the hob over a low heat, add the flour and stir well (it'll be lumpy). Add the wine and salt, then turn up the heat while you keep stirring and the lumps will disappear as it thickens. Add the stock and rosemary and boil some more.

6 Serve the beef with the gravy, the spuds and, if you like, some veggies of your choice.

CORNED BEEF POT PIE

Feeds 4

vegetable oil, for frying

200g (7oz) smoked bacon lardons

1 onion, sliced

1 garlic clove, finely chopped

500g (1lb 2oz) McCartney's of Moira corned beef, cut into 4–4.5cm (1½–1¾in) cubes

6 gherkins, chopped

2 carrots, diced

200ml (7fl oz) bitter (beer)

200ml (7fl oz) beef stock

1 tbsp chopped parsley

1 tsp caster sugar

salt and white pepper

beaten egg, to glaze

4 pieces of ready-rolled puff pastry, cut to fit your individual pie dishes

mashed potato, to serve (optional)

Of all the meats featured in this chapter, the good old corned beef is right up there for me! It has nothing at all to do with corn – it's the rock salt 'kernels' that have become known as 'corn' in the slow process of turning brisket into beautiful corned beef. Now this is a must: go online to www.mccartneysofmoira.com and find somewhere that stocks their corned beef. It's incredible. If you're making this recipe, order double because you'll eat half of it before you even begin cooking. Obviously other CBs work, but if you want a taste of heaven, you know what to do.

1 Preheat the oven to 180°C/fan 160°C/gas mark 4.

2 Heat a little oil in a saucepan and fry the bacon until crisp. Remove and drain on kitchen paper.

3 Add a bit more oil to the pan and fry the onion and garlic for about 5–6 minutes until soft.

4 Add the cooked bacon, corned beef, gherkins, carrots, bitter, beef stock, parsley and sugar to the pan and season well. Bring to the boil, then simmer for 25 minutes. Remove from the heat and let the mixture cool completely. (The mix is cooled before using to prevent the pie lid from getting soggy.)

5 Divide the mixture between 4 individual pie dishes. Brush the edge of each dish with beaten egg, sit a pie lid on top and trim to fit. Brush with the beaten egg and bake for about 20 minutes until the lids are crisp and golden. Serve with mash, if you like.

85g (3oz) plain flour

2 large eggs, beaten

150g (5½oz) breadcrumbs

4 rose veal fillets, about 175–200g (6–7oz) each, battered out to 5mm (¼in) thick

125g (4½oz) butter

1 tbsp olive oil

1 garlic clove, peeled

Salsa verde

1 bunch of flat leaf parsley

½ bunch of mint

½ bunch of tarragon

15g (½oz) anchovy fillets

15g (½oz) capers

15g (½oz) Dijon mustard

lots of olive oil – about 100–150ml (3½fl oz–¼pint)

juice of 1 lemon

salt and black pepper

Sautéed potatoes

100g (3½oz) butter

2 tbsp vegetable oil

about 450g (1lb) baby new potatoes, boiled until tender, then drained and cut in half

1 tbsp white wine vinegar

1 tbsp chopped parsley

salt and black pepper

ROSE VEAL ESCALOPES, SALSA VERDE & SAUTÉED POTATOES

When I first cooked with British rose veal on TV, so many people complained that it was cruel. But, the thing with rose veal is that it's not cruel. It's recommended for eating by so many animal welfare organizations, as the bull calves are looked after in humane conditions rather than slaughtered at birth. Have a little read-up if you're not sure, then cook this delicious meal, which for me is a perfect weekend dinner. I like a glass of Champagne with it… I know, I've changed.

1 For the salsa verde, process the herbs in a food processor until they've all broken down. Add the anchovies, capers, mustard, olive oil and lemon juice and blend until smooth, then season well.

2 For the potatoes, heat the butter and oil in a frying pan and fry the cooked new spuds for about 5 minutes until they're crispy all over. Toss in the vinegar and parsley and season well.

3 Meanwhile, put the flour, eggs and breadcrumbs in 3 separate bowls. Coat each piece of veal in the flour, then in the beaten eggs and finally in the crumbs. Then heat the butter and oil with the garlic clove in a large frying pan, add the veal and fry for 3–4 minutes on each side.

4 Serve the veal on top of the spuds with the salsa verde spooned over.

BUFFALO WINGS WITH APPLE & CELERIAC SLAW

One of my favourite places in the entire world is Seabright Brewery in Santa Cruz, California. Santa Cruz is still a little bit hippy and rough around the edges. Allegedly, Neil Young has a ranch nearby and it has the feeling of '70s California (I imagine). Seabright is a fine place with great, home-brewed beers and good, honest food like burgers and the best wings in the business. I have no idea if this recipe is right for Seabright, but it hits the spot for me every time.

1 Combine all the marinade ingredients in a large non-metallic bowl, then add the wings. Cover and leave to marinate in the fridge overnight.

2 Lift the wings out of the marinade, place on a rack under a hot grill and grill for 6–7 minutes on each side, or until they are cooked through with no trace of pink, basting with the remaining marinade at the start and when you turn 'em, but no later.

3 Meanwhile, put all the slaw ingredients in a bowl and mix well.

4 Serve the wings and slaw with lots of napkins!

Feeds 6

900g (2lb) chicken wings

Marinade

100g (3½oz) hot pepper sauce (Cholula is my fave)
50g (1¾oz) butter, melted
1 tbsp smoked paprika
salt and black pepper

Apple and celeriac slaw

1 head of celeriac, peeled and coarsely grated
3 eating apples, peeled, cored and coarsely grated
½ red onion, finely sliced
1 tbsp chopped parsley
100g (3½oz) mayonnaise
1 tbsp white wine vinegar

BEEF
BOURGUIGNON

The key to this classic is to make sure you've got nice big chunks of beef. If you cut 'em too small, they'll end up like dog meat. Alongside that, make sure the veg isn't cut too thinly. This dish should be robust and hearty – think French farmer rather than French fancy.

Feeds 6

900g (2lb) boneless beef shin, cut into 5cm (2in) cubes
vegetable oil, for frying
100g (3½oz) bacon lardons
1 onion, sliced
1 carrot, sliced
salt and black pepper
30g (1oz) plain flour
30g (1oz) tomato purée
100g (3½oz) butter
300g (10½oz) button or horse mushrooms, trimmed
16 small shallots, peeled
parsley, to garnish
rice or spuds, to serve

Marinade

500ml (18fl oz) red wine
250ml (9fl oz) game stock
1 tbsp thyme leaves
1 bay leaf
1 garlic clove, crushed

1 Combine all the marinade ingredients in a non-metallic bowl and toss in the beef cubes, then cover and leave to marinate in the fridge, ideally overnight but for 2 hours minimum. Lift the beef out of the marinade and pat dry, keeping the marinade.

2 Preheat the oven to 160°C/fan 140°C/gas mark 3.

3 Heat a little oil in a flameproof casserole dish and fry the bacon until crisp. Add the beef and cook until browned and sealed on all sides, then remove both the beef and the bacon from the dish.

4 Add a bit more oil to the dish and gently fry the onion and carrot for about 5 minutes until softened. Put the beef and bacon back in the pan, season and then sprinkle with the flour. Cook, stirring, for 2 minutes.

5 Now add the tomato purée and cook for a good 5 minutes to remove the bitterness, then stir in the reserved marinade. Bring to the boil, stirring, then put the lid on and cook in the oven for at least 2 hours.

6 Meanwhile, melt half the butter in a frying pan and fry the mushrooms until browned. Remove from the pan and repeat with the rest of the butter and the shallots, cooking them very slowly until they caramelize.

7 Strain the sauce from the casserole into a new pan and cook on the hob until reduced by half, then chuck in all the meat and veg (mushrooms and shallots included). Simmer for 5 minutes, then garnish with parsley and serve with rice or spuds.

LIVER & BACON WITH PAPRIKA GRAVY

School dinners = grey liver + lumpy mash + lumpy gravy = disgusting. However, we're all grown-ups now and the ugly liver and her chavvy mates have become slim, tasty and sophisticated. They hang out in cool restaurants and bars and look hot! So move on people and spread the liver love.

1 Heat the oil in a large frying pan, add the butter and when it begins foaming, add the liver and fry for 2 minutes on each side. Remove from the pan and keep warm.

2 Add the bacon to the pan and cook until crisp. Remove from the pan.

3 Add the onion to the pan and cook for 5 minutes. Add 1 tablespoon of the seasoned flour and cook, stirring, for 2 minutes. Then add the tomato purée and cook for 3 minutes to remove the bitterness. Return the bacon to the pan and stir in the stock, Worcestershire sauce and paprika. Bring to the boil, then simmer for 10 minutes.

4 Return the liver to the pan for 1–2 minutes to warm through.

5 Meanwhile, beat the butter, cream and seasoning into the hot mashed spuds. Serve with the liver and its gravy on top, accompanied by your favourite green veggies.

Feeds 4

1 tbsp vegetable oil

50g (1¾oz) butter

450g (1lb) lambs' liver, rinsed, patted dry and cut into decent-sized slices

150g (5½oz) streaky bacon rashers, cut into strips

1 onion, sliced

about 75g (2¾oz) plain flour, seasoned with smoked paprika, celery salt and garlic powder

1 tbsp tomato purée

500ml (18fl oz) strong beef stock

dash of Worcestershire sauce

1 tsp smoked paprika

green vegetables, to serve

Creamy mash

150g (5½oz) butter

1 tbsp double cream

salt and black pepper

500g (1lb 2oz) Maris Piper potatoes, boiled, drained and mashed

91

WINE-COOKED LAMB SHANK WITH APRICOTS

vegetable oil, for frying

4 lamb shanks, about 900g (2lb) each

1 leek, trimmed, cleaned and roughly chopped

4 celery sticks, roughly chopped

2 carrots, unpeeled and roughly chopped

2 onions, unpeeled and roughly chopped

1 garlic bulb, unpeeled

1 bay leaf

1 tbsp thyme leaves

1 tbsp chopped rosemary

500ml (18fl oz) chicken stock

250ml (9fl oz) red wine

150ml (¼ pint) port

100g (3½oz) ready-to-eat dried apricots

buttery mash and green veg, or bulgur wheat cooked in stock, to serve

Slow-cooked meat is right at the top of my list of fave things. I can't get enough of the soft, sticky stuff, with its huge, big flavour and lovely soft texture. Over recent years, the lamb shank has gone from being a relatively unpopular cut to being one of the most desired. The secret is simply to cook it long and slow without interfering too much, then marvel at your skill in lifting it out of the oven.

1 Preheat the oven to 150°C/fan 130°C/gas mark 2.

2 Heat the oil in a large flameproof casserole dish – big enough to take four lamb shanks, and then some – add the shanks, one at a time, and cook until browned and sealed on all sides, then remove from the dish.

3 Add all the veg and garlic to the dish and cook, stirring, for 2 minutes.

4 Add the herbs and put the lamb back in the pan, placing it on top of the veg. Add the stock, wine, port and apricots, which I like to cut in half.

5 Put the lid on and cook the shanks in the oven for at least 2½ hours, but I like to give it at least another 30 minutes on top of that. Serve with mash and green veg or bulgur wheat.

DUCK
WITH DUCK SCRATCHINGS, GOATS' CHEESE & PICKLED RED CABBAGE

Recently I was honoured to host a night at my dear friend Nigel Haworth's excellent Northcote Manor. His Obsession festival has run for many years and my wife Ali and I have been guests for a few, so last year Nige challenged me to walk the walk, rather than talk the talk. Having had maybe one or two champagnes I agreed… only to wake the next morning to a hangover and a promise! Anyway, a year later the night went well, thanks to all at Northcote and to Steve and Eddie from EARLE. This was the main course – I hope you approve.

Feeds 4

4 duck breasts, about 200g (7oz) each
salt and black pepper
vegetable oil, for deep-frying
sea salt, for sprinkling
75g (2¾oz) plain flour
2 large eggs, beaten
125g (4½oz) panko breadcrumbs
300g (10½oz) goats' cheese log, rind removed and beaten until smooth
watercress, to garnish

Pickled red cabbage

vegetable oil, for frying
1 red onion, finely sliced
1 head of red cabbage, finely shredded
1 bay leaf
50ml (2fl oz) white wine
100g (3½oz) demerara sugar
75ml (2½fl oz) red wine vinegar

1 Score the duck skin in a crisscross pattern and season the duck. Place in a hot frying pan, skin-side down, and cook for about 5 minutes until golden. Flip over and cook on the other side for 2 minutes to seal. Remove from the pan and leave to cool.

2 Cut off the skin, then trim away the excess fat from the skin and cut the skin into strips.

3 Half-fill a deep-fat fryer or deep, heavy-based saucepan with vegetable oil and heat to 180°C, or until a small cube of bread tossed into the oil turns golden in about 30 seconds. Deep-fry the duck skin strips until they crisp up, then remove with a slotted spoon, drain on kitchen paper and sprinkle with sea salt.

4 For the cabbage, heat a little oil in a saucepan and fry the onion and cabbage for 3–4 minutes until softened. Add the bay leaf and wine and cook for 2 minutes. Add the sugar and vinegar and cook for 6–8 minutes more to create a sweet 'n' sour sauce for the cabbage.

5 Put the flour, beaten eggs and breadcrumbs in 3 separate dishes. Roll the goats' cheese into 2cm (¾in) balls. Coat in the flour, then the beaten egg and finally in the breadcrumbs. Reheat the pan of oil and deep-fry the cheese balls for 1 minute. Remove with a slotted spoon and drain on kitchen paper.

6 Finish the duck by returning it to the reheated frying pan and cooking skin-side down for a couple of minutes to seal, then flip over and cook for 3 minutes more. Slice the duck and serve with the cabbage, cheese balls and scratchings.

Feeds 4

meat from 2 confit duck legs
  (see page 37)
2 duck breasts, about 200g (7oz)
  each, skinned
125g (4½oz) fresh white breadcrumbs
50g (1¾oz) cooked sliced shiitake
  mushrooms
1 tbsp chopped parsley
1 garlic clove, crushed
1 large egg, beaten
salt and black pepper
vegetable oil, for frying
500g (Ilb 2oz) dried spaghetti

Tomato sauce

100ml (3½fl oz) olive oil
1 onion, finely chopped
1 celery stick, finely chopped
2 garlic cloves, chopped
45g (1½oz) tomato purée
2 x 400g cans chopped tomatoes
100ml (3½fl oz) chicken stock
100ml (3½fl oz) red wine
salt and black pepper
grated Parmesan cheese, to serve

DUCK MEATBALLS

The humble meatball has become the latest thing to be elevated to haute cuisine status. Canned meatballs in tomato sauce are one of my guilty pleasures, often eaten out of the pan with a good splodge of hot sauce. But in my job, I have a duty to explore and create. These fellas are the best meatballs you'll have ever tasted – unless you don't like duck, that is! They are moist, juicy, full of flavour and work well in a sandwich, a salad, a risotto or, as I'm doing here, with pasta and tom sauce (my kids' fave).

1 Pulse the confit duck leg meat in a food processor until smoothish, then pop into a bowl. Do the same with the breasts, but chop them first.

2 Add the breadcrumbs, mushrooms, parsley, garlic, egg and seasoning and mix together with your hands, then roll into about 12 meatballs.

3 Heat a little oil in a frying pan and fry the meatballs for 4 minutes, turning so that they are browned and sealed all over.

4 For the tom sauce, heat the olive oil in a large saucepan and gently fry the onion, celery and garlic for about 5 minutes until soft.

5 Add the tomato purée and cook out for a few minutes to remove the bitterness. Add the tomatoes, stock, wine and seasoning and bring to the boil. Turn the heat right down, half-cover the pan and simmer for about an hour, stirring the sauce every now and again. (If you want a nice smooth sauce, blend in a food processor and pass through a fine sieve before using.)

6 Add the meatballs and cook for 20 minutes more.

7 Meanwhile, cook the spaghetti in a large saucepan of salted boiling water according to the packet instructions until 'al dente'. Drain and serve topped with the meatballs and tom sauce, scattered with Parmesan.

DOUBLE-CUT PORK CHOPS WITH SAUERKRAUT

I've become a big fan of brining and curing over the years – it softens meat, helps the cooking process and stops it drying out. This is a dish I ate in Virginia with my mate Graham Peers, who has the distinction of being a Scouser who lives in the USA (and has done so for over 15 years) with not one hint of a North American accent. As a point of reference, Downtown Virginia has a great pub called the Penny Lane for any travellers looking for a jukebox with 'You'll Never Walk Alone' on it. Oh, and you'll need to get your butcher to double-cut the chops (ie they're twice as thick). My 'sauerkraut' is a quick version of the real thing,

Feeds 2

100g (3½oz) rock salt
50g (1¾oz) caster sugar
1.2 litres (2 pints) water
2 double-cut pork chops, about 225g (8oz) each

I've owned Greens, my veggie restaurant, for over 20 years now and we have a huge customer base from far and wide. But still, after all this time, we can guarantee that at least once a week someone will say, **'I've never eaten a vegetarian meal in my life'**. To be honest, we all have beans on toast, don't we? Cornflakes? Curry and chips? I always think one of the hard things is to cook veggie food that meat eaters will love as well. So this chapter has a selection of crackers that will get everyone excited by veggie food, then you can all book a table at Greens and I can cook for you.

CREAMY BEETROOT MOUSSE WITH CHEESE STRAWS

I've shouted about the joys of beetroot – in sandwiches, roasted, in risotto, curried, raw, pickled – for a long time, but I felt that I wanted to show the more delicate side of my favourite ingredient, and this lovely creamy mousse does the trick. Agar agar is tricky stuff, as it never really sets like a jelly, but it holds a mousse like this in all the right places. Think of this dish as seeing the girl/boy you see at the bus stop who looks pretty plain (the beetroot) suddenly transformed into a vision of fragrant beauty.

Feeds 6

300g (10½oz) double cream
10g (¼oz) agar agar
salt and black pepper
500g (1lb 2oz) cooked beetroot
  (the vacuum-packed stuff is fine)
dash of chilli sauce
juice of 1 lime
100g (3½oz) crème fraîche
100g (3½oz) creamed horseradish
1 tbsp chopped dill

Cheese straws

200g (7oz) ready-made puff pastry
plain flour, for dusting
beaten egg, to glaze
75g (2¾oz) pecorino cheese,
  finely grated
1 tbsp poppy seeds

1 Bring the cream and agar agar to a simmer in a saucepan and season well. Take off the heat.

2 Purée the beets in a food processor until very smooth (use a little of the cream mixture to help if necessary), then add the chilli sauce, lime juice and the rest of the cream mixture and blitz again. Take your time and make it really smooth.

3 Divide the beet mixture between 6 glasses or bowls. Mix the crème fraîche and creamed horseradish together, then stir in the dill. Spoon this cream evenly on top of each mousse and then chill in the fridge until set and ready to serve.

4 Preheat the oven to 200°C/fan 180°C/gas mark 6.

5 For the cheese straws, roll the pastry out on a lightly floured surface to a 15cm (6in) square about 3mm (⅛in) thick, then cut into 1cm (½in) wide strips. Lay on a baking tray and brush with the beaten egg, then sprinkle over the pecorino and poppy seeds. Bake for about 10–15 minutes until golden brown.

6 Serve each chilled mousse with a couple of lovely cheesy straws.

BEETROOT & CELERIAC FILO PIE WITH HONEYED TOMATO SAUCE

Dave Lockwood, my business partner at EARLE, always used to be scared (seriously) of vegetarian food. He thought he'd turn into a bean sprout if he didn't consume the side of a cow every day. But now his food of choice is either our Cheshire cheese sausages or a filo pie. This fella is full of flavour and texture, and will satisfy the most hungry of horses.

Feeds 6–8

150g (5½oz) peeled celeriac, cut into 2.5cm (1in) cubes
150g (5½oz) peeled beetroot, cut into 2.5cm (1in) cubes
olive oil, for drizzling and frying
salt and black pepper
2 onions, sliced
400g (14oz) good-quality feta cheese
450g (1lb) baby spinach
225g (8oz) butter, melted, for brushing
about 15 sheets filo pastry
clear honey, for drizzling

Tomato sauce

100ml (3½fl oz) olive oil
1 onion, finely chopped
1 celery stick, finely chopped
2 garlic cloves, chopped
50g (1¾oz) tomato purée
2 x 400g cans chopped tomatoes
100ml (3½fl oz) vegetable stock
100ml (3½fl oz) red wine
salt and black pepper
1 tbsp ground cinnamon or 2 cinnamon sticks

1 Preheat the oven to 200°C/fan 180°C/gas mark 6.

2 Put the celeriac and beetroot in 2 separate roasting trays, drizzle with oil and season, then roast for about 30 minutes until soft. Remove and turn the oven down to 160°C/fan 140°/gas mark 3.

3 Meanwhile, heat a good glug of oil in a frying pan and slowly fry the onions over a low heat for about 30 minutes until caramelized.

4 For the sauce, heat the oil in a large saucepan and gently fry the onion, celery and garlic for about 5 minutes until soft.

5 Add the tomato purée and cook it out for a few minutes to remove the bitterness. Add the tomatoes, stock, wine, seasoning and cinnamon and bring to the boil, then turn the heat right down and simmer for about an hour, stirring every now and again. (If you want a nice smooth sauce, blend in a food processor and then pass through a fine sieve before using – remove the cinnamon sticks beforehand if using.)

6 When cooked, mixed the celeriac and beets with the caramelized onions, feta and spinach.

7 Brush a 36cm x 24cm (14¼in x 9½in) baking dish with melted butter and then lay 5 sheets of filo inside, brushing each layer with more butter as you go. Add one-third of the veg mixture, then another 5 sheets of filo, buttered. Repeat until all the veg mixture is used up. Finish with the remaining sheets of pastry and lots of butter.

8 Cut crisscross patterns into the top layer of pastry, taking care not to cut all the way through, then bake for 30–40 minutes until the pastry is golden and crisp.

9 Serve a big square of pie with sauce to each person and drizzle over some honey to finish.

SHALLOT TATIN

Feeds 4

about 175g (6oz) ready-made puff pastry

plain flour, for dusting

about 6 banana shallots (you may need more or less, depending on their size)

green salad leaves, to serve (optional)

Caramel

200g (7oz) caster sugar

50ml (2fl oz) water

30g (1oz) butter

1 tsp sea salt crystals

We've all eaten apple tatin, that delicious, rich, buttery caramel dessert, which is particularly good with a glass of Calvados. This dish is probably less well known, but equally delicious. The caramelized shallots are so sweet that I think a good acidic vinaigrette and a simple green salad are all you need with it.

1 Preheat the oven to 200°C/fan 180°C/gas mark 6.

2 Roll out the pastry on a lightly floured surface to 2–3mm ($^1/_{16}$–$^1/_8$in) thick, then cut out a circle slightly bigger than a shallow 22cm (8½in) ovenproof pan.

3 For the caramel, melt the sugar in the pan until it begins to caramelize. Add the water and boil until it's the colour of honeycomb.

4 Take off the heat and beat in the butter and sprinkle on the salt.

5 Peel the shallots, then cut them lengthways and lay on top of the caramel, with the cut sides facing down.

6 Press the pastry circle on top of the pan and bake for 15–20 minutes until the pastry is puffed up and golden brown. Serve with green salad leaves, if you fancy.

AUBERGINE & MUSHROOM 'SHEEP-FREE' SHEPHERD'S PIE

Here's another dish to add to your repertoire of meat-free classics. This has so much depth of flavour, and the barley gives it a lovely chewy texture. I like to serve this with buttered cabbage and mint sauce.

Feeds 4

100ml (3½fl oz) extra virgin olive oil

1 onion, finely chopped

1 garlic clove, crushed

2 aubergines, trimmed and cut into cubes measuring about 3cm (1¼in)

250g (9oz) chestnut mushrooms, trimmed and halved

2 tbsp tomato purée

150ml (¼ pint) red wine

150ml (¼ pint) vegetable stock

2 tbsp cooked pearl barley

6 tomatoes, chopped

1 tbsp chopped rosemary

1 tbsp thyme leaves

85g (3oz) butter

300g (10½oz) potatoes, boiled, drained and mashed

salt and black pepper

1 Heat a little of the oil in a frying or sauté pan over a low heat and gently fry the onion and garlic for about 5 minutes until soft.

2 Add the rest of the oil and the aubergines and cook for 6–8 minutes. Add the mushrooms and cook for 5 minutes, then add the tomato purée and cook it out for 6 minutes to remove the bitterness.

3 Add the wine and stock and bring to the boil, then simmer for 15 minutes. Add the barley, toms, rosemary and thyme and fold in well, then cook for 2–3 minutes. Spoon into a casserole dish.

4 Beat the butter into the hot mash and season well. Spoon on top of the filling, then pop under a hot grill to crisp up.

BOMBAY POTATO PIE

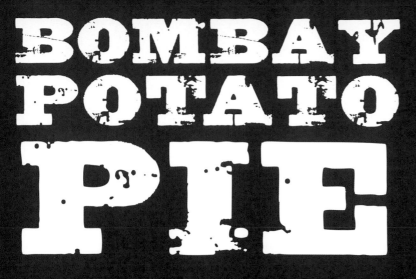

I was having a curry a while ago, tucking into delicious veggie samosas, full of spice and tastiness, and I was thinking how delicious the idea of pastry filled with potato really is – cheese and onion pie, meat and potato pie and the like. Then I wanted to take it further, so I started playing around with a layered pie using filo pastry, like a spanakopita… and this is the result. It's also tasty with a good spoonful of your fave curry sauce on top.

Feeds 6

200ml (7fl oz) vegetable oil

450g (1lb) potatoes, cut into 4cm (1½in) cubes

1 tbsp each coriander seeds and cumin seeds, lightly toasted in a dry frying pan and crushed

1 tbsp garam masala

1 tsp ground ginger

3 red chillies, finely chopped

2 garlic cloves, crushed

salt and black pepper

2 onions, sliced

450g (1lb) baby spinach

100g (3½oz) roasted cashew nuts

1 tbsp chopped fresh coriander

200g (7oz) butter, melted, for greasing and brushing the pastry

about 15–20 sheets of filo pastry

clear honey, for drizzling

To serve
natural yogurt
diced cucumber
sesame seeds

1 Preheat the oven to 180°C/fan 160°C/gas mark 4.

2 Heat 100ml (3½fl oz) of the oil in a flameproof, ovenproof dish. When smoking, add the spuds and shake a little. Add all the spices, chillies and garlic and season well. Roast for about 25 minutes until the potatoes are soft, then leave to cool.

3 Meanwhile, heat the rest of the oil in a frying pan and slowly fry the onions over a low heat for about 30 minutes until caramelized. Leave to cool.

4 Mix the Bombay spuds with the caramelized onions, spinach, cashews and coriander in a bowl.

5 Brush a 36cm x 24cm (14¼in x 9½in) baking dish with melted butter and then lay 3 sheets of filo on top, brushing each layer. Add one-third of the veg mixture, then another 3 sheets of filo, buttered. Repeat until all the veg mixture is used up (make sure you push the mixture into the corners). Finish with the remaining sheets of pastry and lots of butter, then drizzle over some honey.

6 Cut crisscross patterns into the top layer of the pastry, taking care not to cut all the way through, then bake for about 30–40 minutes until the pastry is golden and crisp.

7 Serve the pie with an extra drizzle of honey, topped with a dollop of yogurt and scattered with diced cucumber and a few sesame seeds.

Feeds 6

50g (1¾oz) butter

450g (1lb) Arborio rice

splash of white wine

900ml (1⅔ pints) vegetable stock,
  kept warm in a saucepan

handful of basil, finely chopped

100g (3½oz) sun-dried tomatoes,
  chopped

5 spring onions, finely chopped

salt and black pepper

1 large egg, beaten

50g (1¾oz) plain flour

vegetable oil, for deep-frying

Creamy tapenade

100g (3½oz) pitted black olives

100g (3½oz) SunBlush tomatoes,
  chopped

2 garlic cloves, peeled

finely grated rind and juice of 1 lemon

1 tbsp chopped parsley

100g (3½oz) mayonnaise

ARANCINI WITH CREAMY TAPENADE

When a more mature lady once said in Greens, 'Last time I was in I had some of Simon's tasty little balls', I knew I'd done something right with my arancini. I do love arancini with mozzarella in the middle, but with the creamy tapenade served to accompany these tasty little beauties, I prefer no cheese for balance. You can also make these in advance and chill them until you're ready for ball action.

1 Melt the butter in a heavy-based saucepan. Add the rice and cook for a couple of minutes over a low heat, stirring. When the rice starts to become a little translucent around the edges, add the wine and cook for another minute.

2 Add a ladleful of warm stock (it must be warm to enable the rice to cook properly) and cook over a medium heat, stirring, until nearly all the liquid is absorbed. Continue doing this until all the stock is used and/or the rice is tender.

3 Fold in the basil, sun-dried toms and spring onions and season well. Let the rice cool.

4 Meanwhile, in a food processor, blend all the tapenade ingredients except the mayo together until smooth, then fold in the mayo.

5 Put the beaten egg and flour in 2 separate dishes. Roll the rice mixture into small, ping-pong-sized balls, 3–4cm (1¼–1½in) in diameter, then coat in the egg and then the flour.

6 Half-fill a deep-fat fryer or deep, heavy-based saucepan with vegetable oil and heat to 160°C, or until a small cube of bread tossed into the oil turns golden in about 45 seconds. Deep-fry the arancini, in batches, for 3 minutes, then remove with a slotted spoon and drain on kitchen paper. Serve with the tapenade.

BROAD BEAN & COURGETTE PILAF

It's believed that this tasty Persian dish has been around since the 10th century, originally using barley. I find the heady combination of flavours just divine. Be brave when you make it and go even bigger on the spices than the recipe says – it'll drive you wild.

1 Heat the oil in a saucepan and gently fry the onion and garlic for about 6–8 minutes until soft. Add all the spices and cook, stirring, for 3 minutes.

2 Stir in the rice, broad beans and stock, cover and cook over a low heat for 12–15 minutes until the rice is tender. Stir in the butter.

3 Meanwhile, brush the courgette slices on both sides with oil and season. Add to a hot griddle pan and cook for 3 minutes on each side until charred.

4 Spoon the rice into bowls and top with the courgette pieces, then garnish with chopped parsley and mint, lemon wedges and Greek yogurt.

Feeds 6

50ml (2fl oz) vegetable oil, plus extra for brushing

1 onion, finely chopped

2 garlic cloves, crushed

2 tsp each cumin and coriander seeds, lightly toasted in a dry frying pan and ground with a mortar and pestle

10 cardamom pods

2 cloves

1 cinnamon stick

1 tsp turmeric

225g (8oz) basmati rice, soaked in cold water for 20 minutes and drained

200g (7oz) podded broad beans

400ml (14fl oz) vegetable stock

50g (1¾oz) butter

4 courgettes, trimmed and cut into 3cm (1¼in) thick rounds

salt and black pepper

To garnish

chopped parsley and mint

lemon wedges

Greek yogurt

CRISPY PANCAKES WITH LEEK & STILTON

When I was a kid I used to love those Findus Crispy Pancakes with beef mince in 'em. The crispy crunch followed by sloppy, boiling hot mince was a treat no child could resist. One day, at a menu meeting at Greens, we started chatting about them and wondered if we could do a modern version of them… and, oh yes, we could. This is one of the most popular dishes we've ever made at Greens. Obviously, feel free to change the filling, but make sure you burn your mouth on the first taste – them's the rules.

Feeds 6

3 large eggs, beaten
200g (7oz) polenta
vegetable oil, for deep-frying

Pancakes

100g (3½oz) plain flour
pinch of salt
2 large eggs
200ml (7fl oz) milk
75ml (2½fl oz) water
50g (1¾oz) butter, melted
vegetable oil, for frying

Leek and Stilton filling

100g (3½oz) butter
2–3 leeks, trimmed, cleaned and cut
  into half-moons (nice and thin)
½ onion, diced
1 garlic clove, crushed
1 tbsp thyme leaves
salt and black pepper
300g (10½oz) Stilton cheese, crumbled

1 For the pancakes, sift the flour and salt into a bowl, then make a well in the centre and break the eggs into it.

2 Whisk the eggs into the flour then, little by little, whisk in the milk and water – add the liquid slowly to avoid lumps. Finally, whisk in the melted butter.

3 Get some oil really hot in an 18cm (7in) frying pan, then turn the heat down to medium. Spoon about 4 tablespoonfuls of batter into the pan, then swirl it around the pan to get an even covering. After about 30 seconds, flip the pancake over and cook the other side. Remove from the pan and repeat with the rest of the batter, adding more oil as necessary, to make more pancakes, stacking 'em up with greaseproof paper between until you're ready to use them.

4 For the leek and Stilton filling, melt the butter in a frying or sauté pan and gently fry the leeks, onion and garlic for about 8 minutes until soft. Take off the heat, add the thyme and season well, then scatter in the Stilton. Leave to cool.

5 When both the filling and pancakes are cool, divide the filling between the pancakes and roll each into a tight sausage.

6 Brush the rolls with the beaten eggs, then roll in the polenta. Half-fill a deep-fat fryer or deep, heavy-based saucepan with vegetable oil and heat to 180°C, or until a small cube of bread tossed into the oil turns golden in about 30 seconds. Deep-fry the rolls, in batches, for 5–6 minutes until crispy. Remove with a slotted spoon and drain on kitchen paper.

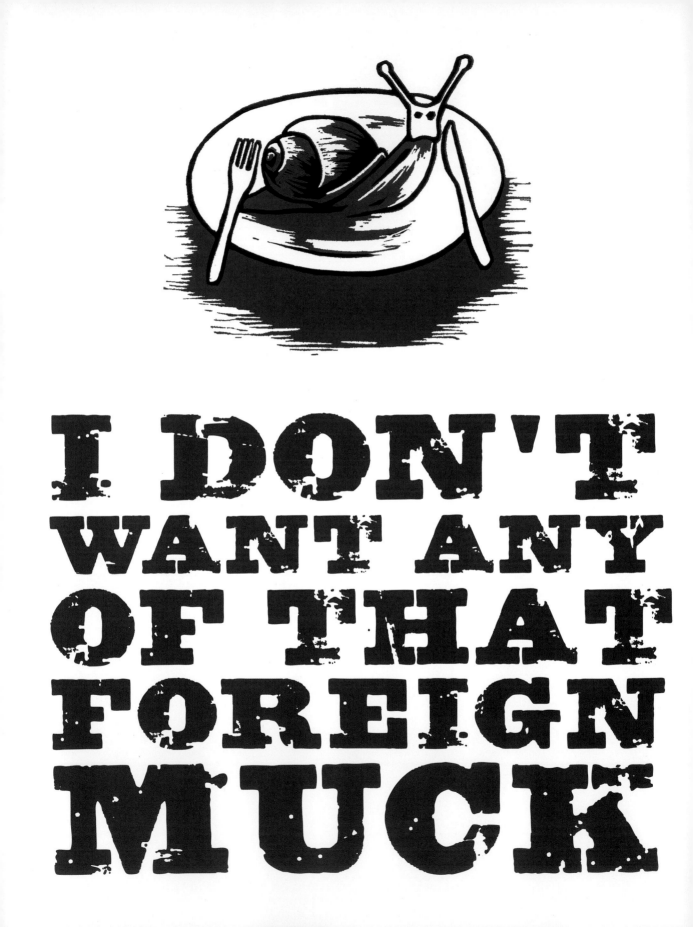

I DON'T WANT ANY OF THAT FOREIGN MUCK

My best friend in the world, Martin Hodgson, lives in Bangkok and has done for many years. We went over to visit him a while ago and went for lunch at the stunning Oriental Hotel on the bank of the river. Sitting on the next table was an elderly British lady who was having a very heated discussion with the waiter about the menu. Whatever he suggested wasn't good enough and she actually said to the incredibly patient waiter, 'Young man, **I don't want any of that foreign muck'**. Brilliant. So, if you, too, don't want any of that foreign muck, skip this chapter, as it's full of it.

RABBIT & SNAIL PAELLA

My great uncle Pepe was born in Valencia and it's a city that I've fallen in love with. I adore driving past the paddy fields on the way to the city, then sampling many of the 365 different paellas that are supposed to exist. I did a number at a beautiful restaurant there, about eight years ago, where they still cook on open flames using the wood of orange grove trees. The heat under the tin roof, as we piled on more wood to fire it up, was overwhelming. The old guy, Juan, revealed his 'secret' ingredient, which was a good tablespoon of finely chopped rosemary to aromatize the rice – joyous. P.S. I can't mention Valencia without telling you about a bar called Johnny Maracas – the best bar ever. Go very late and behave disgracefully for me!

Feeds 6

about 50ml (2fl oz) olive oil

150g (5½oz) chorizo, cut into large chunks

1 onion (Spanish, of course), diced

1 red pepper, cored, deseeded and sliced

2 garlic cloves, sliced

pinch of dried chilli flakes

500g (1lb 2oz) Calasparra rice (use risotto rice if you can't find it)

1 tbsp thyme leaves

1 tbsp finely chopped rosemary

1 tsp paprika

pinch of turmeric

75ml (2½fl oz) white wine

4 tomatoes, chopped

500ml (18fl oz) chicken stock

salt and black pepper

1 rabbit, jointed

150g (5½oz) fresh or drained canned snails

100g (3½oz) fresh or frozen peas

To serve

bread
garlic mayonnaise
lemon wedges

1 Preheat the oven to 180°C/fan 160°C/gas mark 4.

2 Heat half the oil in a flameproof casserole dish and fry the chorizo until crisp, then turn the heat down, add the onion, red pepper, garlic and chilli flakes and cook for 3–4 minutes.

3 Add the rice, herbs, paprika and turmeric and stir well, then add the wine and cook for 2–3 minutes.

4 Add the toms and stock to the casserole, then stir well and season. Pop in the rabbit pieces, add the lid and cook in the oven for 25 minutes until the rabbit is cooked through and the rice is tender.

5 Remove the casserole from the oven, stir in the snails 'n' peas and return to the oven for 4 minutes more. Serve the paella with bread, garlic mayo and lemon wedges.

BUFFALO RENDANG

Feeds 4

juice of 2 limes, plus extra limes
  to serve
pinch of caster sugar
pinch of salt
500g (1lb 2oz) boneless buffalo
  shoulder, cut into large cubes
vegetable oil, for frying
200g (7oz) block of coconut cream
50g (1¾oz) desiccated coconut,
  toasted
400ml can coconut milk

Spice paste

2 onions, chopped
4 garlic cloves, peeled
125g (4½oz) tamarind paste
2.5cm (1in) fresh root ginger, peeled
4 red chillies
15g (½oz) curry powder
10g (¼oz) ground coriander
1 tsp turmeric
1 lemon grass stalk
a little salt

To serve

jasmine rice
chopped coriander

Located just over the border in North Wales, John Sigsworth and his family keep magnificent buffaloes. The farm is beautiful and the meat is juicy and full of flavour. I was filming there a while ago, and as I was in the field delivering my lines about local produce, rare breeds and what have you, walking slowly towards the cameraman, I was suddenly aware of a tension in the air. As I was walking, one of John's buffaloes had become very interested in me and was making progress just a little too quickly towards me. We all froze, unsure what to do. I turned to face my potential attacker… as the beast ambled to the left to munch on a particularly juicy patch of grass. Funnily enough, we didn't go for a second take. Rendang is a great dish – a rich, long, slow cook used to break down the tough fibres in the meat. It may seem like a big time commitment, but it really is worth it.

1 Combine the lime juice, sugar and salt in a non-metallic bowl and stir in the meat. Cover and leave to marinate in the fridge for at least 45 minutes.

2 Put all the paste ingredients in a food processor and blend until smooth.

3 Heat a little oil in a large flameproof casserole dish or heavy-based saucepan and fry the meat until browned and sealed all over. Remove from the pan.

4 Heat some more oil in the pan until hot but not smoking, then fry the spice paste until fragrant, taking care not to burn it.

5 Cut thin slices of the coconut cream off the block and add to the pan a little at a time. Add the toasted desiccated coconut and then gradually add the coconut milk. Bring the sauce to the boil and put the meat back in the pan.

6 Cook the rendang over a low heat for about 2 hours – the aim is to reduce the sauce to a thick paste that coats the meat (but if it goes too far, just add a little water to loosen it). Serve with jasmine rice and coriander.

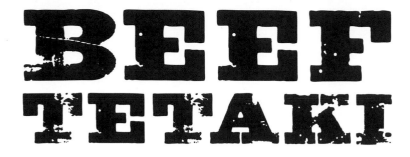

BEEF TETAKI

I like Japanese food more and more. There's something lovely about the fresh, simple, intense flavours. With my love for sushi, I've also become a bit of a media tart recently. A good few years ago I was filming in the middle of Lancashire with a very posh director for a corporate video, and the young runner was charged with getting lunch. So we all accepted the location and shrugged that any kind of remotely edible butty would be fine. But the director actually asked, 'What kind of sushi do you think you could get?' FACT! Problem is, I think I'd be asking that now… I've changed.

1 Rub oil all over the beef and season. Add to a large hot frying pan and cook until browned and sealed on all sides. Remove from the pan.

2 Mix all the marinade ingredients together in a bowl. Add the meat to this, rub in the marinade and transfer all of it to a sealable plastic bag. Seal and leave to marinate in the fridge for at least 2 hours.

3 When ready to serve, whisk all the dressing ingredients together in a bowl. Arrange the salad ingredients on plates and spoon over the dressing.

4 Slice the chilled meat very thinly and arrange on the salad – this is lovely presented on a board as a help-yourself salad.

Feeds 4

vegetable oil, for rubbing
500g (1lb 2oz) piece of beef fillet
salt and black pepper

Marinade

2 tbsp vegetable oil
75ml (2½fl oz) soy sauce
50ml (2fl oz) rice vinegar
1 banana shallot, finely sliced
2 tbsp soft dark brown sugar
finely grated rind of 1 lime
5cm (2in) piece of fresh root ginger, peeled and grated
2 garlic cloves, sliced

Wasabi dressing

50ml (2fl oz) soy sauce
50ml (2fl oz) rice vinegar
1 tbsp soft dark brown sugar
1 tsp wasabi paste
finely grated rind and juice of 1 lemon
1 red or green chilli, finely chopped

Salad ingredients

bean sprouts
watercress
sliced cucumber
sliced shallot
pickled ginger

Feeds 6

vegetable oil, for frying

800g (1lb 12oz) thick-cut pancetta, cut into 3cm (1¼in) squares

3 onions

400g can haricot beans, drained and rinsed

400g can butter beans, drained and rinsed

75g (2¾oz) muscovado sugar

50g (1¾oz) dark molasses or black treacle

50g (1¾oz) tomato ketchup

6 cloves

1 garlic clove, sliced

1 tbsp Dijon mustard

1 tsp paprika

1 tbsp plus 2 tsp sherry vinegar

salt and black pepper

1 tbsp chopped parsley

crusty buttered bread, to serve (optional)

BOSTON BAKED BEANS

Whatever you've got planned for tea tonight, abandon those plans and make this instead! I can't think of a better dish to make for any occasion. Boston baked beans are posh baked beans with pancetta, mustard and other yummy ingredients. Now, do they originate from Boston? I'm not sure. I first had them in New York sitting at a counter in a diner on 7th Avenue with a malted vanilla shake. It's a big old eat, but if you want to go XL, a few good-quality sausages thrown in makes it something that should probably be illegal.

1 Preheat the oven to 160°C/fan 140°C/gas mark 3.

2 Heat a little oil in a flameproof casserole dish and fry the pancetta until just beginning to crisp. Remove from the pan.

3 Peel the onions and cut into quarters, leaving the base on so that they hold together. Add a bit more oil to the pan and fry the onions for about 5–6 minutes until they're nicely coloured.

4 Put the pancetta back in the pan with everything else except the parsley, mix well and season. Add the lid and bake in the oven for about 1½ hours, stirring occasionally (if it begins to dry out, add a little water).

5 Stir in the parsley, season well and serve with crusty buttered bread.

LAMB SAAG BALTI

Curry, or Indian curry in reality, is probably the meal of choice for my family. Poppadums, followed by a selection of bhajis, samosas and tandoor faves, then assorted treats including chicken tikka masala, dopiaza, bhuna – you name it. In fact, everything apart from this, lamb saag balti. My Ali just doesn't like it – doesn't like the texture of the spinach nor the big deep flavour. So I can guarantee that whenever I'm out with my mates, I will ALWAYS have it. Cook it long 'n' slow for maximum depth, and don't forget to buy a few cheeky bottles of Kingfisher to pop in the fridge.

1 In a food processor, blend the onion, garlic, ginger and chillies together until smooth.

2 Heat the cumin and coriander seeds in a dry pan until lightly toasted, then grind with a mortar and pestle.

3 Heat a little oil in a heavy-based saucepan or flameproof casserole and fry the lamb until browned and sealed all over. Remove from the pan.

4 Add a bit more oil to the pan and fry the onion mix for a good 15 minutes to evaporate the liquid and brown but not burn it.

5 Put the lamb back in the pan, add the spices, toms and stock and bring to the boil, then turn the heat down and simmer for at least 45 minutes.

6 Stir in the spinach and cook for 10 minutes more. Serve with all the goodies… and one of those cold Kingfishers you bought.

Feeds 4

1 onion, roughly chopped

3 garlic cloves, peeled

2.5cm (1in) piece of fresh root ginger, peeled and chopped

2 (or 3) green chillies, chopped

1 tbsp cumin seeds

1 tbsp coriander seeds

vegetable oil, for frying

750g (1lb 10oz) boneless lamb shoulder, trimmed and cut into big chunks

2 cardamom pods, crushed

1 tsp turmeric

6 tomatoes, chopped

300ml (½ pint) strong lamb stock

250g (9oz) spinach, chopped

To serve
rice
coriander leaves
lime wedges

COQ AU VIN

There's always been a place in my heart for a delicious dish of coq au vin. When I was a kid I thought anything French was posh food, so I was excited when I finally tried this delicious bowl of loveliness. And, of course, it's not posh! It is a great rich, deep chicken stew/casserole that could warm Anglo–French relations in a flash.

1 Melt 15g (½oz) of the butter in a large flameproof casserole dish or heavy-based saucepan and gently fry the bacon for 5 minutes – don't let it burn. Remove from the pan.

2 Season the pieces of bird, add to the pan, in batches, and cook until the skin is golden all over but not too brown. Remove from the pan.

3 Add another 15g (½oz) butter to the pan and fry the onion, carrot, celery and garlic for about 8 minutes until softened. Put the bird pieces and bacon back in the pan, sprinkle with the flour and cook, stirring, for 2 minutes. Stir in the wine, Cognac and herbs.

4 Ladle ln the hot stock until the bird pieces are covered. Bring to the boil, then turn right down, half cover and let the casserole gently bubble for 30 minutes, or until the chicken is cooked through.

5 Meanwhile, melt the remaining butter in a frying pan and slowly fry the baby onions or shallots and button mushrooms until golden, then add them to the casserole.

6 Once the bird bits are cooked, lift them out and boil the sauce until thick and glossy, then pop the chicken back in. Serve with rice.

Feeds 2

75g (2¾oz) butter

150g (5½oz) smoked bacon lardons

salt and black pepper

1 large chicken, about 2.5kg (5lb 8oz), jointed into 6 or 8 pieces

1 onion, sliced

1 large carrot, sliced

2 celery sticks, chopped

2 garlic cloves, sliced

30g (1oz) plain flour

75cl bottle red wine – a big red Burgundy would be lovely

2 tbsp Cognac

2 bay leaves

few sprigs of thyme

400ml (14fl oz) good hot chicken stock

12 baby onions or shallots

200g (7oz) baby button mushrooms

rice, to serve

CHICKEN CHOW MEIN

Saturday night was chippy tea night at our house when I was a kid. The best Chinese takeaway was called Tsang's just down the road from ours, and to this day I've yet to eat a more delicious curry sauce, despite years of trying. So Tony, if you're reading this… PLEEEEEEEEEEASE! The food was so good that you'd have to queue out on to the street, but it was always worth it. But my other fave was chicken chow mein, and what set Tsang's apart was using cooked chicken, shredded, rather than stir-frying it raw. Alongside my version is a delicious sticky aubergine dish that complements the chow mein brilliantly.

Feeds 4

sesame and vegetable oil, for stir-frying

2 spring onions, sliced, plus extra to serve

2.5cm (1in) piece of fresh root ginger, peeled and cut into matchsticks

1 garlic clove, sliced

1 red pepper, cored, deseeded and finely sliced

2 tbsp light soy sauce

1 tbsp good-quality dark soy sauce

175g (6oz) cooked egg noodles

2 cooked skinless chicken breasts, about 200g (7oz) each, cut into thin matchsticks

1 tsp cornflour (if needed to thicken)

1 tsp Chinese five-spice powder

150g (5½oz) bean sprouts, rinsed

Sichuan pepper, to garnish

Sticky aubergines

75ml (2½fl oz) groundnut oil

3 aubergines, trimmed, peeled and cut into 2cm (¾in) thick slices

5cm (2in) piece of fresh root ginger, peeled and cut into matchsticks

3 garlic cloves, sliced

50g (1¾oz) soft brown sugar

125ml (4fl oz) Chinese rice wine

125ml (4fl oz) water

50ml (2fl oz) light soy sauce

25ml (1fl oz) black rice vinegar

1 red bird's eye chilli, chopped, plus extra to serve

1 Heat a mixture of sesame and vegetable oil in a wok until smoking hot, add the spring onions, ginger and garlic and stir-fry for 1 minute.

2 Add the red pepper, then both soys, the noodles and the chicken. Keep cooking and stirring for 5 minutes to fully heat through (if it looks a little wet, mix the cornflour with a tablespoon of cold water to make a paste, add to the pan and cook, stirring, until the sauce thickens). Transfer to a serving dish and keep warm.

3 For the aubergines, heat the groundnut oil in the wiped-out wok, then add the aubergines, ginger and garlic and stir-fry for 3 minutes. Add the sugar and keep stirring for 30 seconds. Add the rice wine, water, soy, vinegar and chilli and cook for 3 minutes.

4 Spoon the aubergines into a bowl and serve with the chow mein, garnished with Sichuan pepper and chopped chilli and spring onions.

BAKED CUBAN-SPICED CHICKEN WITH RICE

Of all the recipes in this fine book, I will guarantee this will be the one that you cook more than any other. My nephew Peter (12) has claimed this as his own, making it for friends and family at any given opportunity. The thing is, it's sooooo simple, you won't believe how it can taste this good. If you don't like spices, you can do this without the spice mix and it still tastes like the best chicken dish ever.

1 Preheat the oven to 180°C/fan 160°C/gas mark 4.

2 Blend all the spice mix ingredients together with the oil in a bowl.

3 Melt a little of the butter in a frying pan and fry the chicken until golden. Remove from the pan.

4 Add the sausage, carrots, onion and garlic to the pan and cook for about 8 minutes until the vegetables are soft and the sausage is browned.

5 Mix the vegetables with the rice, toms, beans, the rest of the butter and the spice mix, then season.

6 Put half the rice mixture in a well-buttered casserole dish, sit the chicken in the middle, then top with the rest of the rice. Mix the booze into the stock, then pour this over the rice. Put on the lid and bake in the oven for about 30 minutes until the rice is cooked.

7 Garnish with parsley and serve with chilli sauce or garlic mayo.

Feeds 4

100g (3½oz) butter, plus extra for greasing

350g (12oz) skinless chicken breast, cut into big chunks

125g (4½oz) spicy sausage, such as merguez, chorizo or Polish, chopped

2 carrots, sliced

1 onion, sliced

1 garlic clove, crushed

350g (12oz) short-grain rice

4 tomatoes, roughly chopped

400g can mixed beans, drained and rinsed

salt and pepper

50ml (2fl oz) Cuban rum

1.5 litres (2¾ pints) chicken stock

1 tbsp chopped parsley, to garnish

chilli sauce or garlic mayo, to serve

Spice mix

2 tsp dried oregano

2 tsp ground cumin

2 tsp paprika

2 tsp soft dark brown sugar

2 tsp garlic powder

2 tsp onion powder

salt and white pepper, to taste

a little vegetable oil, for blending

COD WITH PROVENÇALE LANGOUSTINE STEW

I do cookery demos all over the country and the various food festivals I attend show the wealth of incredible produce we have in the British Isles. Always a good one to go to is Aberdeen's Taste of Grampian food festival, a one-day event in the local cattle market, packed full of lovely people and producers. The pre-festival dinner is always a riot with ritual ribbing of the guests, last time myself, Jean-Christophe Novelli and Scotland's First Minister Alex Salmond, who challenged me to get the word 'baldy' into my show, and I did! One of the producers, GMR Seafoods, gave me some smoked langoustine tails, which are, quite possibly, one of the greatest things I've ever eaten. So if you can, get some, but if not, add a little well-smoked bacon to this stew.

Feeds 4

4 thick-cut cod loin fillets, about 175g (6oz) each
100g (3½oz) plain flour, seasoned with salt and black pepper
olive oil, for frying
knob of butter
juice of ½ lemon

Provençale langoustine stew

175ml (6fl oz) extra virgin olive oil
1 red onion, sliced
1 garlic clove, finely chopped
150ml (¼ pint) red wine
24 tomatoes, skinned
1 tbsp black olives
250g (9oz) smoked langoustine tails
1 tbsp chopped tarragon

1 For the stew, heat a little of the oil in a saucepan and gently fry the onion and garlic for 5 minutes until softened.

2 Add the wine, turn up the heat and cook to reduce by half. Stir in the toms, then drop the heat down again and simmer for 15 minutes (add a little water if the stew dries out).

3 Add the rest of the oil, the olives and langoustine tails and cook for 5 minutes, then stir in the tarragon.

4 Meanwhile, dust the cod with the seasoned flour. Heat a glug of oil in a frying pan, add the fish, skin-side down, and fry for 4 minutes, then flip over and cook for 4 minutes more until just cooked through. Add the butter and baste the fish, then squeeze over the lemon juice. Serve on top of the stew.

BABY SQUID STUFFED WITH CHILLI PRAWN RICE

I've never been the biggest fan of barbecue, if I'm honest – too many rubbish burgers and burned sausages, and enough raw chicken to last a lifetime. But a while ago I did some work with Calor Gas and really got excited by the possibilities, so this is a variation on the barbecue theme, where the squid stays deliciously chewy, giving way to sticky risotto rice.

1 For the rice, melt the butter with the oil in a saucepan and fry the onion, garlic and chilli for 4 minutes until softened. Add the rice and stir to coat well with the buttery mix.

2 Breaking with tradition, add half the stock and the fish sauce and bring to the boil, then simmer for about 12 minutes, stirring occasionally. Once most of the stock is absorbed, stir in the prawns. Now add the rest of the stock, a ladleful at a time, cooking and stirring until it's mostly absorbed before adding the next, until the rice is cooked – the aim is for it to be stickier than in a risotto. Stir in the coriander and leave to cool.

3 Pack the cooled rice into the squid tubes and seal the top of each with a cocktail stick. Rub with oil and cook over a hot charcoal or gas barbecue, or in a hot griddle pan, for about 6 minutes in total, turning regularly. Garnish with coriander and serve with delicious fresh toms.

Feeds 6

12 baby squid tubes, cleaned
vegetable oil, for rubbing
fresh tomatoes, to serve

Chilli prawn rice

50g (1¾oz) butter
1 tbsp olive oil
1 onion, finely diced
1 garlic clove, crushed
1 red chilli, finely diced
300g (10½oz) Arborio rice
400ml (14fl oz) chicken stock, kept warm in a saucepan
1 tbsp fish sauce
175g (6oz) cooked peeled baby prawns, chopped
1 tbsp chopped coriander, plus extra to garnish

A MUCKMENT OF SAUCE

My mum's a great cook; her lasagne is the dish of legends, her apple pie the taste of my childhood. But sometimes when we're in restaurants she will speak her mind… and some. One of her pet hates is food swamped in what she describes as **'a muckment of sauce'**. Now that can be anything from a divine red wine reduction to a cloying creamy sauce. It's a great expression that she uses all the time, without realizing it. So this chapter is all about the muckment of sauces and dressings that you need in your culinary wardrobe to bring out for the right occasion.

BLACK VINEGAR DRESSING

Makes about 250ml (9fl oz)

handful of coriander
100ml (3½fl oz) black vinegar
100ml (3½fl oz) vegetable oil
3 tbsp dark soy sauce
1½ tbsp sesame oil
2 red bird's eye chillies, finely chopped
1 tbsp sesame seeds

Chinese black vinegars are quite simply delicious. They have a rich, malty, sugary, spicy flavour, and I love 'em with chicken, fish or rare beef. This dressing is dead simple, and by mixing it with natural yogurt you'll get another equally stunning version.

1 Finely chop the coriander and then mix with everything else. (If you make big batches of this, keep checking the flavour each time you use it to ensure that it doesn't become too sour.)

PERI-PERI MAYO

Makes about 300g (10½oz)

10 red bird's eye chillies
100ml (3½fl oz) olive oil
juice of 1 lemon
2 tbsp garlic powder
1 tsp salt
1 tsp paprika
pinch of caster sugar (if needed)
250g (9oz) mayonnaise

I don't remember the modern Western world BN – Before Nando's. It's the only fast-food chain that I love, with its grilled chicken, rice, coleslaw and sauces to blow your mind – what's not to like? As a chef, I always want to know how to make things I taste, and Nando's Peri-Peri Sauce is near the top of that list. This is not a bad attempt at it, but when it gets mixed with the mayo… well, you'll get it – it's a kicker.

1 Blend everything except the mayo together in a mini food processor or blender until very smooth (you can add a pinch of sugar if the chillies are too bitter).

2 Mix with the mayo, adjust the consistency with water and dip in chips, chicken, sausages… or just your fingers!

DUKKAH

Dukkah is an Egyptian creation, and the name comes from the Arabic verb 'to pound'. It can be used as a dry spice mix, a rub, a sauce or a condiment... in fact, this is possibly the most multi-functional recipe in the book! Below is my fave mix but, as ever with my recipes, you should take ownership and twist it your way. The dry mixture is delicious – use it as a spice mix, or serve it with extra virgin olive oil and bread; adding the wet bits changes it again – this version is great spooned on top of grilled white fish.

1 For the dry mixture, heat the fennel, coriander and cumin seeds with the cloves gently in a dry frying pan until lightly toasted, then grind with a mortar and pestle until smooth.

2 Combine with the paprika, chilli flakes, turmeric, hazelnuts, pistachios and sesame seeds and mix well.

3 Alternatively, to make a wet mixture, just before cooking, mix together the spice seeds and cloves with the honey, oil, orange juice and seasoning.

Enough for 4 servings

1 tsp fennel seeds
1 tsp coriander seeds
1 tsp cumin seeds
½ tsp cloves
1 tsp paprika
½ tsp dried chilli flakes
pinch of turmeric
50g (1¾oz) blanched hazelnuts, chopped
30g (1oz) pistachio nuts, chopped
1 tbsp sesame seeds

To cook (optional)
4 tbsp clear honey
4 tbsp olive oil
juice of 1 orange
salt and black pepper

135

RED WINE VEGETABLE RAGU

Makes about 500ml (18fl oz)

olive oil, for frying
2 onions, finely chopped
3 carrots, finely chopped
4 celery sticks, finely chopped
1 garlic clove, crushed
200g (7oz) tomato purée
200ml (7fl oz) red wine (a soft Merlot
  is good)
200ml (7fl oz) strong vegetable stock
2–3 sprigs of rosemary

Of all the recipes in this book, this could be the most useful. It can be used as the basis for a Bolognese, chilli or lasagne. It's also a tremendous vegetarian sauce that works in stews and casseroles, and has a richness that will satisfy even the most devout of carnivores. Oh and it's also yummy with a simple bit of fish, meat or a juicy banger sitting on top of it. Make lots of it and freeze what you don't need.

1 Heat a good splash of oil in a saucepan and fry all the vegetables and garlic for about 10 minutes over a low heat – this will release a lot of sweetness and make a delicious base.

2 Now add the tomato purée. Cook this out for a good 8 minutes to remove all bitterness and bring a richness to the sauce.

3 Add the wine, stock and rosemary and bring to the boil. Stir well, then drop the heat right down and simmer for at least 45 minutes, but a good 1½ hours will make a sauce that really blows your mind.

Makes about 500ml (18fl oz)

vegetable oil, for frying

3 onions, sliced

1 garlic clove, sliced

200g (7oz) tomato purée

225ml (8fl oz) strong vegetable stock

75ml (2½fl oz) Madeira

50ml (2fl oz) gravy browning (optional, but great for colour)

500ml bottle Robinsons Unicorn Bitter, or something similar

1 tbsp caster sugar (optional)

salt and black pepper

50g (1¾oz) butter, chilled and cubed

BEST-EVER VEGGIE GRAVY WITH ROBINSONS BITTER

Feel free to make this a non-veggie gravy – the addition of beef, chicken or game stock is all it needs. But one of the best things to be able to make for a non meat-eater is a gravy that's this tasty. Now I'm using Unicorn Bitter from my good friends at Robinsons brewery in Stockport, but feel free to use your own local brew. As a muckment of sauce expert, I think you'll love this.

1 Heat a glug of oil in a saucepan and fry the onions and garlic for about 5 minutes until softened.

2 Add the tomato purée and cook it out for at least 6–8 minutes to remove the bitterness.

3 Add all the liquids, including the browning if you like, and bring to the boil, then boil for about 20 minutes. Add the sugar if you'd like to soften the flavour, and season well.

4 Now blend the gravy really, really well in a food processor – you can pass it through a sieve afterwards, if you like, but if you blend it for ages you won't need to.

5 Once it's blended, return the gravy to the pan over a low heat and whisk in the butter for a glossy finish.

VINDALOO

Remember the first time you went for an Indian curry? The aim was to see who could eat the hottest dish off the menu and, while the Tarkka (cue bad joke – like a vindaloo but a little 'otter) and Pharl were available, the vindaloo was the dish of choice. The ones I ate – at curry houses fed up of ignorant gangs of people thinking that's all there was to Indian food – were mostly rubbish, so it was all heat and no taste. Well, when you have a proper vindaloo, it will blow your mind for all the right reasons, as it's full of heat and full of flavour – deep and rich.

1 For the paste, simply blend all the ingredients together in a small food processor or blender until they're smooth – the longer you blend it for the better.

2 For the 'marinade', again simply blend all the ingredients together.

3 The way this works is to either fry the paste gently for 5 minutes in a little vegetable oil, then add the 'marinade' to make a yummy sauce, or use the marinade to marinate the meat (lamb, chicken, beef or venison) overnight, then cook the whole lot, meat 'n' paste, long and slow. Either way, it's delicious.

Makes about 20 servings

Curry paste

1 garlic clove, peeled

2.5cm (1in) piece of fresh root ginger, peeled

8 red chillies

1 tsp ground cinnamon

1 tsp ground cumin

1 tsp ground coriander

pinch of turmeric

50ml (2fl oz) malt vinegar

50ml (2fl oz) warm water

Vindaloo 'marinade'

1 tsp black peppercorns, crushed

3 green chillies

100ml (3½fl oz) malt vinegar

50ml (2fl oz) red wine

2 tsp caster sugar

8 cardamom pods

8 cloves

salt

THE PASTRIES
ARE
ASSUMED

What is it about the Irish that makes them such superb storytellers? Two of my friends, Martin and Maurice, are from the Emerald Isle and can talk the hind legs off a donkey. On a football weekend in Barcelona, they swapped stories about the family 'tour' that they do every time they get back from a trip. Every aunt, cousin and gran lays on a 'spread'; to refuse is a sign of 'becoming English'! Tea and a 'wee pastry' are compulsory at every stop. As the stories got more elaborate, Maurice talked of a relative who would bring out homemade pies, sandwiches and a vast array of savoury goodies. I asked, 'What about the sweet stuff?', to which Maurice replied, **'the pastries are assumed'**. I feel the same about sweet things in a cookery book.

BRANDY SNAPS WITH HAZELNUT CREAM

I remember being at my auntie's house as a little kid, sitting on her rocking chair listening to her whistling away in the kitchen. Next thing, she appears with the most magnificent-looking cakes in the world! Yes, people, I'd been introduced to the brandy snap, cheekily luring me with their glossy, lean outsides and whipped-cream-packed insides. Well, it's enough to tempt any young man, and I've never looked back. You can all make your own, wrapping 'em around any kind of cylinder that has a diameter of about 2cm (¾in), but a wooden spoon is customary. They really are wicked temptresses and the hazelnut cream is pure filth.

Feeds 4

115g (4oz) butter
115g (4oz) caster sugar
4 tbsp golden syrup
2 tbsp brandy
115g (4oz) plain flour
1 tsp ground ginger
vegetable oil, for oiling
seasonal fresh fruit, to serve

Hazelnut cream

300ml (½ pint) double cream
1 vanilla pod, split lengthways and seeds scraped out
100g (3½oz) Nutella or any hazelnut spread

To decorate

icing sugar, for dusting
finely chopped hazelnuts

1 Melt the butter, sugar and syrup with the brandy in a saucepan. When they're combined, take the mixture off the heat.

2 Mix the flour and ginger together, then fold into the butter mixture. Cover and chill.

3 Preheat the oven to 180°C/fan 160°C/gas mark 4.

4 Line 2 large baking trays with baking parchment. Roll the brandy snap mixture into balls about 2cm (¾in) across and drop four balls on each baking tray, about 10cm (4in) apart. Bake for 5–7 minutes until molten and bubbling, then remove from the oven and leave to cool slightly. Meanwhile, oil the handle of a wooden spoon or your cylinder of choice.

5 Carefully loosen each brandy snap from its paper with a palette knife, then wrap it carefully around the spoon handle to form a cylinder. Slide the snap off the end of the spoon and leave to cool and crisp up.

6 Whip the cream, vanilla seeds and hazelnut spread together, spoon into a piping bag fitted with a medium plain tube, then pipe into the cooled brandy snaps. Dust with icing sugar, scatter with chopped hazelnuts and serve with seasonal fresh fruit.

Feeds 6

Raspberry brownies

300g (10½oz) plain dark chocolate with 70% cocoa solids

250g (9oz) butter, softened, plus extra for greasing

4 large eggs, beaten

200g (7oz) caster sugar

150g (5½oz) soft light brown sugar

125g (4½oz) plain flour

25g (1oz) cocoa powder

½ tsp baking powder

pinch of salt

100g (3½oz) fresh raspberries

Caramelized banana sauce

125g (4½oz) soft dark brown sugar

125g (4½oz) butter

125ml (4fl oz) double cream

12 bananas

The mess

300ml (½ pint) double cream

2 tbsp icing sugar

1 vanilla pod, split lengthways and seeds scraped out

125g (4½oz) Greek yogurt

12 meringue nests, broken into smallish bits

RASPBERRY BROWNIE & CARAMELIZED BANANA ETON MESS

This is for my beautiful daughter, Flo. Like most teenagers she's fussy about her food, but if ever I need to win her round or treat her, this is the way to do it. Here I'm using shop-bought meringues and making my own brownies, but feel free to swap that, or make 'em both or buy them both. Whichever way you decide, this is DE-LISH-US.

1 Preheat the oven to 180°C/fan 160°C/gas mark 4. Grease and line a 32cm x 23cm (12¾in x 9in) baking tin.

2 For the brownies, melt 200g (7oz) of the chocolate, broken into pieces, with the butter in a heatproof bowl set over a saucepan of barely simmering water (make sure the water doesn't touch the bottom of the bowl), then leave to cool. Chop the rest of the choc.

3 Beat the eggs and sugars together in a large bowl for 5 minutes until the mixture is pale and fluffy. Gently sift in the flour, cocoa powder, baking powder and salt and fold in with a large spoon, then fold in the melted choc, followed by the chopped choc and the raspberries.

4 Spoon the mixture into the prepared baking tin and bake for 35 minutes, or until crispy to the touch and fudge-like on the interior (a skewer inserted into the centre should come out with a skim of the mixture attached). Leave to cool.

5 Meanwhile, put all the caramelized banana sauce ingredients except the bananas in a saucepan and boil for 5–6 minutes until a rich, thick consistency develops. Leave to cool slightly, then chop the bananas into the sauce.

6 For the mess, whip the cream with the icing sugar and vanilla seeds until you have soft peaks, then fold in the yogurt.

7 Now for the assembly. I like to make a massive bowl of this, but feel free to divide it between individual sundae glasses instead. So I chop up the brownies into 2.5–3cm (1–1¼in) pieces and gently fold them and the meringues into the whipped cream mixture, then swirl in the banana sauce so that it looks rippled. Eat too much, then lie down in a darkened room.

SOFT CHOCOLATE-CENTRED BANANA PUDDING

Makes 6

225g (8oz) butter, softened, plus extra for greasing
400g (14oz) caster sugar
1 vanilla pod, split lengthways and seeds scraped out
4 large eggs
300g (10½oz) self-raising flour
250ml (9fl oz) milk
4 ripe bananas, mashed
ice cream, to serve

Ganache

175ml (6fl oz) double cream
1 tbsp caster sugar
150g (5½oz) plain dark chocolate with 70% cocoa solids, broken into pieces

Sauce

200g (7oz) golden syrup
100g (3½oz) butter
100g (3½oz) soft light brown sugar

We've all eaten those lovely chocolate fondant desserts made with very little flour so that when you press the spoon into the pud all the gooey chocolate sauce oozes out. Well, this recipe is based on that, but it's a traditional sponge style with chocolate ganache in the middle, which will be gooey, if not oozy.

1 For the ganache, heat the cream and sugar together in a saucepan to just below the boil, then pour over the chocolate pieces in a bowl. Mix well to melt the choccy, then chill to set.

2 For the puddings, preheat the oven to 180°C/fan 160°C/gas mark 4. Grease 6 dariole moulds, ovenproof cups or individual ramekins.

3 Beat the butter, sugar and vanilla seeds together in a bowl for 3–4 minutes until the mixture is fluffy. Add the eggs, one at a time, beating well after each addition. Mix in about a third of the flour, then half the milk, another third of the flour, the rest of the milk and finally the rest of the flour. Quickly fold in the bananas.

4 Spoon the mixture into the greased dishes, filling them halfway up. Roll the now-set ganache into 6 balls about 2.5cm (1in), then drop one into the middle of each dish and top up with the rest of the pudding

mixture. (You'll have a bit too much ganache, so roll the rest into balls, then roll in cocoa powder and make choccies for your... self!)

5 Stand the dishes in a roasting tin and pour in enough water to come halfway up their sides. Cover with foil and bake for about 25–30 minutes until the puddings are set.

6 Meanwhile, for the sauce, bring the ingredients slowly to the boil and cook until the sugar has melted.

7 To serve, turn the puddings out of their dishes on to serving plates, using a palette knife to loosen them around the edges. Pour over the sauce, add a scoop of ice cream, cut open and scoff.

PEAR & ALMOND CAKE

Because my mate Maurice is such a granny when it comes to pastries, I want to have just made this cake for him next time he comes knocking on my door. It has the sweetness of a tarte tatin, the moistness of a Victoria sponge cake and that little hint of sharpness from the caramel flavour. Come on Maurice, I've even got the pastry forks out!

1 Preheat the oven to 180°C/fan 160°C/gas mark 4. Grease and line a 23cm (9in) round cake tin.

2 Melt 100g (3½oz) of the butter with the Marsala in a saucepan. Sprinkle the brown sugar over the base of the prepared tin, pour over the melted butter mixture, then add the pears – arrange them in a pretty overlapping pattern if poss.

3 Beat the rest of the butter and the caster sugar together in a bowl for about 5 minutes until pale and fluffy. Now beat in the eggs, one at a time.

4 Mix all the dry ingredients together in a separate large bowl, then fold the eggy mixture into them, followed by the yogurt. Spoon this mixture on top of the pears.

5 Bake the cake for 1 hour–1 hour 20 minutes until a skewer inserted into the centre comes out clean.

6 Leave to cool a bit, then invert on to a plate. Serve with loads of naughty clotted cream.

Feeds 8

300 g (10½oz) butter, plus extra
 for greasing

50ml (2fl oz) Marsala

175g (6oz) soft dark brown sugar

4 ripe pears, peeled, cored and cut into
 2cm (¾in) thick slices

300g (10½oz) caster sugar

3 large eggs

225g (8oz) plain flour

90g (3¼oz) ground almonds

1½ tsp baking powder

1 tsp ground cinnamon

250ml (9fl oz) natural yogurt

clotted cream, to serve

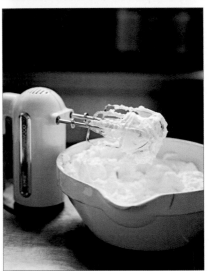  

JAFFA CAKE CHEESECAKE

In our house, Jaffa Cakes are the relatively okay choccy biccy that my Hamish eats as a treat/sugar hit before football. He read in a footy mag that a lot of professional players will have the odd JC. So when it was his birthday, I decided to use that idea in a real treat way, and this cake is the result. It's a bit of a lengthy process making it – you let the sponge cool, make the cheesecake, cook, let it cool, make the jelly, cool, cut it out, make the ganache, pour over, let it set – but it's really worth it, I promise.

Feeds 10

4 large eggs
100g (3½oz) caster sugar
100g (3½oz) plain flour

Chocolate cheesecake

200g (7oz) plain dark chocolate, broken into pieces
500g (1lb 2oz) full-fat cream cheese
500g (1lb 2oz) ricotta cheese
25g (1oz) caster sugar
6 large eggs, beaten
75g (2¾oz) cocoa powder

Marmalade jelly

1 tbsp orange marmalade
125ml (4fl oz) boiling water
135g pack orange jelly

Ganache

200ml (7fl oz) double cream
150g (5½oz) golden caster sugar
200g (7oz) plain dark chocolate with 70% cocoa solids, broken into pieces
20g (¾oz) butter

1 Preheat the oven to 180°C/fan 160°C/gas mark 4. Grease and line a 25cm (10in) round springform cake tin.

2 Put the eggs and caster sugar in a heatproof bowl set over a saucepan of simmering water (make sure the water doesn't touch the bottom of the bowl) and whisk with a hand-held electric whisk for 5 minutes.

3 Take the bowl off the heat, then gently sift in the flour and fold in well with a large spoon. Spoon into the prepared tin and bake for about 12 minutes until springy to the touch. Leave to cool completely in the tin.

4 For the chocolate cheesecake layer, melt the choc in a heatproof bowl set over a saucepan of barely simmering water (again, make sure the water doesn't touch the bottom of the bowl), then leave to cool.

5 Preheat the oven again to 180°C/fan 160°C/ gas mark 4. Pulse the cheeses and sugar in a food processor until smooth. Mix in the eggs, then the cocoa and melted choc.

6 Spoon on to the sponge base and bake for about 1 hour until springy to the touch. Leave to cool completely in the tin.

7 For the jelly, mix the marmalade and boiling water together and cut the jelly into cubes. Add to the water and stir until dissolved, then pour into a baking tray – you want the jelly to be about 1cm (½in) deep – and leave until set. When cool, cut a 20cm (8in) circle of the jelly (use a plate as a guide) and sit it on top of the cheesecake (which should still be in its tin).

8 For the ganache, bring the cream and sugar to just below the boil in a saucepan, then pour over the choc and butter in a bowl and stir well until both have melted. When the ganache has cooled slightly, pour over the cheesecake and chill to set.

Take note – you need to allow each stage to cool completely before starting the next.

butter, for greasing
4 large eggs
100g (3½oz) caster sugar
100g (3½oz) plain flour
chocolate sauce and cream,
  to serve

Blackcurrant mousse

400g (14oz) blackcurrants
150g (5½oz) caster sugar
75ml (2½fl oz) crème de cassis
6 gelatine leaves
3 tbsp hot water
150ml (¼ pint) double cream,
  lightly whipped
50ml (2fl oz) Greek yogurt
2 large egg whites

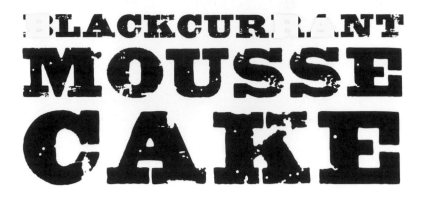

BLACKCURRANT MOUSSE CAKE

I've always loved the expression that we eat with our eyes. This delicious cake deserves a place on a cake trolly. It looks like a weird pretend cake with its majestic colouring. If it's not blackcurrant season, then raspberries also work quite wonderfully.

1 Preheat the oven to 180°C/fan 160°C/gas mark 4. Grease and line a 20cm (8in) springform or loose-bottomed cake tin.

2 Put the eggs and sugar in a heatproof bowl set over a saucepan of simmering water (make sure the water doesn't touch the bottom of the bowl) and whisk with a hand-held electric whisk for 5 minutes.

3 Take the bowl off the heat, then gently sift in the flour and fold in well with a large spoon.

4 Spoon the sponge mix into prepared tin and bake for 8–10 minutes until springy to the touch. Cool briefly, then release from the tin, remove the lining paper and leave to cool completely on a wire rack.

5 For the mousse, put the fruit, sugar and booze in saucepan and cook for 4–5 minutes. Meanwhile, dissolve the gelatine in the hot water.

6 Purée the fruit in a food processor, then add the gelatine, cream and yogurt and blend until smooth. Pour into a bowl.

7 Whisk the egg whites in a separate bowl until you have stiff peaks, then fold into the fruit mix. Spoon on to the sponge base and chill overnight. Serve with choccy sauce and cream.

APPLE & STRAWBERRY COBBLER

I remember as a kid being on holiday in Anglesey having our tea out somewhere and eating an apple cobbler. I thought that the café had simply made a really bad crumble, nice but no more. Only as a grown-up did I realize that the rubbish crumble top was actually a delicious cobbler. The topping can be a little sticky, so enjoy being a kid when you make it, or get your kids to make it with you. To be a bit wacky, crumble Cheshire cheese on to the cobbler before cooking.

Feeds 6

350g (12oz) cooking apples, peeled, cored and chopped

350g (12oz) eating apples (Cox's or Braeburn), peeled, cored and chopped

175g (6oz) caster sugar

1 cinnamon stick

200g (7oz) strawberries, hulled and halved

warm custard, to serve

Cobbler topping

225g (8oz) plain flour

3 tsp baking powder

pinch of salt

25g (1oz) demerara sugar

100g (3½oz) butter, chilled and cubed

175ml (6fl oz) buttermilk or soured cream

1 Preheat the oven to 200°C/fan 180°C/gas mark 6.

2 Put the apples, sugar and cinnamon stick in a saucepan and cook over a low heat for 8–10 minutes until soft, then add the strawberries and remove the cinnamon stick.

3 For the cobbler, in a food processor, pulse together the flour, baking powder, salt, sugar and butter. When it looks like breadcrumbs, add the buttermilk or soured cream and pulse again. The dough will be very sticky.

4 Spoon the fruit mixture into a shallow 25cm (10in) ovenproof pan or a medium-sized baking dish, then add 'blobs' of the cobbler all over, leaving gaps for the fruit to ooze up. Bake for about 25 minutes until the cobbler is risen and nicely browned. Serve with warm custard.

COCONUT RUM 'N' RAISIN CAKE WITH COCONUT CUSTARD

Feeds 8

butter, for greasing
4 large eggs, separated
200g (7oz) caster sugar
200g (7oz) plain flour
1 tsp baking powder
1 vanilla pod, split lengthways and
  the seeds scraped out
100ml (3½fl oz) milk
150g (5½oz) desiccated coconut
100g (3½oz) raisins, soaked in rum

Coconut custard
6 large egg yolks
125g (4½oz) caster sugar
40g (1½oz) plain flour
400ml can coconut milk

I sat on my massive balcony in Antigua, staring at the ocean as I was about to go and do a cookery demo for some lovely Brit holidaymakers, and I thought, 'Where did it all go wrong?' It was one of those incredible moments that make me pinch myself – some chancer from Merseyside who's blagged his way on to a trip to Antigua 'cos he's on telly, and all I had to do was cook a few Caribbean-inspired dishes. So then I reached down, picked up my plate and had just one more dainty morsel of this cake, which I'd cooked as a trial in the afternoon before making it at my demo. So when you eat this, think of me in Antigua, because probably right now I'm in South Manchester, chopping onions.

1 Preheat the oven to 180°C/fan 160°C/gas mark 4. Grease and line a 23cm (9in) square baking tin.

2 Beat the egg whites in a large bowl until you have stiff peaks. Gradually fold in the sugar, a tablespoonful at a time, then the yolks, one at a time.

3 Combine the flour, baking powder and vanilla seeds in a bowl. Make a well in the centre, pour the milk into it and whisk into the flour, then quickly fold into the egg mixture. Stir in 100g (3½oz) of the coconut. Squeeze out the excess rum from the raisins (keep this) and fold them in too.

4 Bake the cake for about 30–40 minutes until a skewer inserted into the centre comes out clean. Pour over the rum from the raisins, plus a little extra if you fancy, then sprinkle over the rest of the coconut.

5 For the custard, whisk the egg yolks and sugar together in a bowl until pale and thick, then sift in the flour and mix well. Bring the coconut milk to the boil in a saucepan, then immediately pour it on to the egg mixture and stir well. Pour back into the pan and return to the boil. Turn the heat down and cook for another 5 minutes until it thickens (if it gets too thick, add some cream or milk). Serve the cake with a glug of custard.

Feeds 6

225g (8oz) plain flour

1 tsp bicarbonate of soda

225g (8oz) caster sugar

100g (3½oz) mini marshmallows

65g (2¼oz) butter, plus extra for
  greasing

75ml (2½fl oz) vegetable oil

3 tbsp cocoa powder

200ml (7fl oz) cola

100g (3½oz) buttermilk or soured
  cream

2 large eggs, beaten

To serve

creamy custard or Greek yogurt

fresh raspberries

FIZZY COLA CAKE

I scoffed a version of this cake in New York a couple of years ago. It was one of those times when you don't really like the idea of something but figure, in the interests of research, that you should try it. Well, it's incredible! The cola (use your brand of choice, but not the diet variety) adds a lovely gentle caramel flavour and a sticky feel, like a good ginger cake.

1 Preheat the oven to 180°C/fan 160°C/gas mark 4. Grease and line a 25cm (10in) round cake tin.

2 Sift the flour and bicarbonate of soda into a bowl and stir in the caster sugar and mini marshmallows.

3 Bring the butter, oil, cocoa powder and cola to the boil in a saucepan. Pour the mixture over the dry ingredients and mix well, then add the buttermilk or soured cream and the eggs and mix until just combined.

4 Pour into the prepared tin and bake for 45 minutes–1 hour until a skewer inserted into the centre comes out clean. The cake will be deliciously sticky and is incredible served with creamy custard or Greek yogurt and scattered with fresh raspberries.

INDEX

THANKS

I've so many people I need to mention who have made this book the very personal thing it is. I want it to be as exciting as getting the new *Scorcher* annual always used to be for me when I was young. So a big thanks to everyone connected with making the book, especially Yasia, Eleanor, Alice, Lesley and Emma; also thanks to Anne Kibel and Laura Hill for looking after me like a king; my right-hand girl Claire, McCartney's of Moira for being corned beef makers extraordinaire; Lee Frost for the meat; everyone at my restaurants Greens and EARLE, including Steve, Nick, Simon, Bob and Dave; I'd like to mention the whole dining experience at Azurmendi in Bilbao for making me rethink my entire life in food; of course all my mates for being the greatest source of hilarity – Martin (3), Maurice, Frew, the Irish lot, Sull, Dib, Scho and the LFC lot, Scotty and Babs; all the telly lot – Tim, Seb, Claire, Yaz, Dave Sk, Jay, Emma and Hen; and finally my brilliant family – Ali, Flo, Hamish, Mum, Dad, Jane, Ettore and Peter for humouring me.